How to Work for Peace

■ ■ ■

How to Work for Peace

David W. Felder

■ ■ ■
Florida A&M University Press
Tallahassee

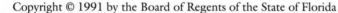
Library of Congress Cataloging in Publication Data

Felder, David W.
  How to work for peace / by David W. Felder.
    p. cm.
  Includes bibliographical references and index.
  ISBN 0–8130–1071–3 (alk. paper)
  1. Peace movements. 2. Peace. I. Title.
JX1952.F39 1991   91–17817
327.1'72—dc20   CIP

■ ■ ■

To my wife, Judy, and to the memory of Norman Cousins

Contents

II.
Outlawing War 23

III.
Providing Security 57

Acknowledgments

Epigraphs on part title pages come from the following sources:

Part I. Ruth Benedict, *An Anthropologist at Work: Writing of Ruth Benedict* (London: Secker & Warburg, 1959), p. 370.

Part II. Alfred Lord Tennyson, "Locksley Hall," in *The Works of Tennyson,* edited by Lord Tennyson Hallam (New York: Macmillan Company, 1935), pp. 98–99.

Part III. Albert Einstein, *Einstein on Peace* (New York: Simon and Schuster, 1960), p. 407.

Part IV. William Blake, "A Poison Tree," in *Songs of Experience* (London: Author and Printer W. Blake, 1794; reproduced from a copy at the British Museum; London: Ernest Benn Ltd., 1927), p. 14.

Part V. H.G. Wells, *The Outline of History: Being a Plain History of Life and Mankind* (New York: P. F. Collier and Son Company, 1922), vol. IV, p. 1305.

Part VI. Alfred North Whitehead, *Dialogues of Alfred North Whitehead as Recorded by Lucien Price* (Boston: Little, Brown and Company, 1954), p. 100.

Artwork on part title pages comes from the following sources and is used with permission:

Part I. "The Small Society" comic strip by Brickman. Reprinted with special permission of King Features Syndicate, Inc.

Part II. From *My Fellow Americans* by Ron Cobb with permission from Price/Stern/Sloan Inc., Los Angeles.

Part III. "Ground Zero," copyright 1982 by John Trever, *Albuquerque Journal,* reprinted with permission of John Trever.

Part IV. Oliphant copyright 1989 Universal Press Syndicate. Reprinted with permission. All rights reserved.

Part V. "In the Laboratory of Human Affairs," Daniel R. Fitzpatrick. Reprinted with permission of the *St. Louis Post-Dispatch*.

Part VI. "Hi and Lois" comic strip reprinted with special permission of King Features Syndicate, Inc.

Introduction

The message of this book is that peace is possible. Everyone is aware of the dangers of a continued arms race and the proliferation of nuclear weapons. Now people want solutions. *How to Work for Peace* starts where other books leave off. *How to Work for Peace* is a book with solutions.

The solution is to abolish war by establishing enforced international law. In part I, I argue that the peace movement must provide a positive alternative to the Strategic Defense Initiative so that its opposition to the SDI is more than support for the current policy of deterrence. If we define peace in a sensible manner—not as the ending of all conflicts, but as the nonviolent resolution of conflict between nations—we see that a system of law can provide an alternative to war.

In part II, I examine institutional structures that have been established for settling conflicts between nations. There are at least two models for the abolition of war. We might have nations give up little bits of their sovereignty in well-defined areas, as is being done in the European Community, or we might work for a World Federation analogous to the United States. I examine organizations that propose outlawing war and the objections to this proposal.

Here you will find the story behind the headlines. It is a story of how some people have changed their thinking because of nuclear weapons, and of others who do not understand the need to change. The old way of thinking assumed that military superiority provides political benefits and that military alliances provide security. The new way of thinking assumes that superior weapons cannot provide benefits in the nuclear age and that no nation can be secure unless all nations are secure within a system of common security. One cannot understand the development of the European Community, the debate on the future of NATO and the Warsaw Pact, arms control talks, or the war in the Persian Gulf without understanding the contrast between the old and new ways of thinking.

In part III, I detail how the nuclear age began with the assumption that military superiority bestowed political benefits. When people started to realize that nuclear weapons were different because they could not use them, they started to change their thinking. The Anti-Ballistic Missile (ABM) treaty stated that neither side would attempt to defend itself against nuclear attack. This assumed the common security viewpoint that either all nations will be secure or no nation will be secure. Then U.S. leaders embraced the Strategic Defense Initiative, a defense system. I conclude part III with a discussion of the contrast between national defense and common security.

In part IV, I contrast maintaining the current system of military alliances with establishing a system of common security. The continuation of the process of change in the Soviet Union and in Eastern Europe depends on creating new security arrangements in Europe. I discuss ways to encourage positive change, including citizen diplomacy.

The solution I advocate—strengthening global institutions— cannot work without the development of a planetary consciousness. In part V, I discuss ways we can foster a global consciousness so that individuals see themselves as members of a global community in addition to being citizens of nations. In this section I consider peace studies and provide sample lessons in conflict resoluton and game theory.

In part VI, I discuss how we can be effective in working for peace and I explore actual things one might do, including working with community peace groups and supporting national legislation. I list things one can do that take only minutes a day, and outline how to tell whether actions for peace are effective. In the final chapter, I examine how the concepts developed in this book apply to situations we confront in countries like Nicaragua, Grenada, and Panama, and to Iraq's invasion of Kuwait. The war in the Persian Gulf illustrated the choice between attempting to provide security through military alliances, such as the one the United States has with Saudi Arabia, and transforming the United Nations into a system of common security.

It is time that those interested in peace sought a solution to the war problem. Discovering what has to be done does not by itself solve any problems, because solutions sometimes require ingredients that are not attainable. But no problems can be solved when actions are not related to the solution. Thinking about a solution can help us to aim our efforts.

I believe that world peace is an attainable goal. Further, I believe that anyone who asks the relevant questions will come to the same conclusion.

Part I

Thinking about Peace

HOW DID WE EVER
GET INVOLVED IN
ANYTHING AS STUPID
AS OVERKILL?

UNDERTHINK—

7-2
BRICKMAN

Reprinted with permission of King Features Syndicate, Inc.

■ War is an old, old plant on this earth, and a
natural history of it would have to tell us
under what soil conditions it grows, where it
plays havoc, and how it is eliminated. Control
of war cannot be based on anything less than
such knowledge, and until our efforts are thus
grounded despair is premature.
—Ruth Benedict

1

■■■

What Does the Peace Movement Offer?

■■■

There is a difference between a peace movement and an antiwar movement. An antiwar movement focuses on ending involvement in one conflict and ends when that one conflict ends. A peace movement focuses on the abolition of war and succeeds only when war no longer exists. The main challenges the peace movement faces are to convince people that war can be abolished and to motivate people to take the necessary steps.

It is time for the peace movement to have a program, instead of the usual pattern in which the government proposes and the peace movement opposes. The government intervened in Vietnam and in the Persian Gulf and the peace movement opposes military interventions. Whenever the government proposes new weapons systems, the peace movement opposes them.

While it certainly is the role of a peace movement to oppose acts of war and escalations of the arms race, it is not enough just to oppose government actions. More than opposition is needed, for example, to respond to the Strategic Defense Initiative, the "Star Wars" initiative introduced in a televised speech on March 23, 1983, in which President Reagan rejected the policy of deterrence that had guided the arms race. Instead of weapons aimed at population centers, Reagan proposed tactical weapons aimed at other weapons. Because the peace movement also rejects the policy of Mutual Assured Destruction, it is not enough just to oppose the Star Wars proposal. If we want our opposition to be more than support for the status quo, we must propose alternatives to both the Strategic Defense Initiative and Mutual Assured Destruction.

The peace movement must also provide an alternative to President George Bush's New World Order. It is not clear what the new order is supposed to be, but it is clear that the existing order that allows nations to wage war must be changed. Those who opposed the Persian Gulf War must explain how they would stop an aggressor. If we do not want to see the United States act as the world's policeman, we must propose an alternate world order.

Need for a Positive Peace Movement

To be successful a movement must state what it is for, as well as what it is against. A positive peace movement focuses on building institutions for peace and the advantages of those institutions, rather than simply pointing out the dangers of nuclear war. Because the positive is more satisfying psychologically than the negative, a successful movement for peace must be built on more than stressing fear and criticizing existing security arrangements. Confronted with information on the horror of nuclear weapons, people try to shut the information out. They give in to despair rather than rise to action. Only by focusing on a solution can we go beyond the paralyzing effect of the negative.

One can take positive and negative actions for peace. (Both may be called for, so I am not criticizing one by calling it negative and praising another by calling it positive.) Negative actions include those aimed at decreasing the military actions of one's government. Positive actions include those aimed at creating a climate in which no one will want to use military force.

Traditionally, peace movements have placed their main emphasis on trying to get nations to reduce their weapons. I would like to see a new emphasis on moving toward a structure of peace. Building a structure of peace only indirectly involves removing the structure of war. If peace is established, then preparations for war cannot be justified.

A peace movement should have both positive and negative aims. The positive aim is to build a structure of peace, and the negative aim is to remove the structure and weapons of war. That the positive and negative aims of the peace movement are separate can be illustrated by an example. People can work to build international institutions while leaving the military machinery of each country intact, and people can also work to reduce military preparedness while doing nothing to build international structures that might provide a nonviolent alternative to war.

Peace Movement and Antiwar Movement

One difference between an antiwar movement and a peace movement is that an antiwar movement succeeds when a particular war ends, but a peace movement succeeds only when people no longer expect wars to occur. With an antiwar movement, one takes sides— one opposes the actions of one's own government. With a peace movement, one tries to take an international outlook and to avoid placing blame. The emphasis is not on supporting one side or the other, but on helping to create new ways of interacting.

Before the movement against the war in Vietnam, the peace movement was larger. Two of the largest groups, Turn Toward Peace and Students for Peace, were concerned with the abolition of war. I was first exposed to the peace movement when I heard Robert Pickus, national coordinator of Turn Toward Peace, speak in 1962 in my hometown on the topic "Building Support for Alternatives to War: Brookline's Role in a New Approach." Within a few years the peace movement had been swallowed up by the antiwar movement, and they both collapsed when the war in Vietnam ended. Now with the end of the Persian Gulf War, the antiwar movement that opposed United States intervention will lose members.

Both an antiwar movement and a peace movement might oppose military interventions in areas such as Vietnam and the Persian Gulf, but they do so in different ways. An antiwar movement tries to get one country to withdraw its troops, while a peace movement tries to get all countries to use and strengthen international peace institutions like the World Court and the United Nations. The end result that an antiwar movement hopes to achieve is the withdrawal of troops, with the expectation that it might be a little easier to organize an antiwar movement against the next war. A peace movement strives to have conflicts resolved by the use of international institutions in order to establish a habit of using those institutions.

A Solution to the War Problem

At the risk of sounding outrageous I will make a strong claim—peace is as simple as one, two, three: one, recognize that peace is concerned with conflict between nations; two, recognize that peace requires only the resolution of conflict and not its removal; three, recognize that enforceable international law would provide a method of resolving conflicts between nations.

The goal of those working toward peace is an effective peace movement able to contribute to providing an alternative to war. I believe that the peace movement is not effective, partly because it does not articulate a positive alternative to war, and partly because it chooses inappropriate targets to criticize.

Difficulties in Working for Peace

It is not easy to work for peace. You have to worry about whether what you are doing will really help to achieve your objective. Also, you have to worry about being misunderstood. There are those who will distort what you are doing because in their own limited vision they picture the world in terms of the war system and cannot envision that you are working to bring about another way for human beings to settle their conflicts.

Certain types of actions are less likely than others to be misunderstood. Some actions are traps that make it hard for us to posit a peace alternative, while others are relatively free from problems.

As I examine various policies, I ask that you judge them as effective if people outside the peace movement can understand them, and as traps if they are actions that present no alternative to those we should be trying to convince—those who believe that there is no alternative to planning for war. Such a person is not necessarily a person who likes war. One may believe that no one likes war, but that wars are nevertheless a necessity and preparation for war a national duty.

Suppose we make military spending our target and argue that money currently spent on weapons should be spent on hospitals, education, and other social needs. Suppose we point out that the country cannot really afford to spend on weapons. These arguments will not persuade people who think that it is necessary to be prepared for war, because, unless they are convinced that there is an alternative to war, they will believe that they have a duty to be prepared. Those who believe weapons are needed may reply that it is unfortunate that money must be spent on weapons, but it has to be. They may see the problem of budget deficits, but, once again, it cannot be helped. They may even be proud that, despite the costs, the country has the fortitude to stick to its defense spending.

Pressures to control defense spending have had an effect on defense policies. After World War II, the United States had a choice: match the Soviet forces in Europe or rely on nuclear weapons. It is partly because the American public did not want to pay for conventional weapons that the United States started to build its nuclear arsenal. Nuclear weapons were much cheaper than paying for more troops. The main effect of complaints about military spending has been to make the United States rely on nuclear weapons.

I think that military spending is an inappropriate target for those who want peace. The costs of military defense will not and should not dissuade governments from spending money on arms. If people feel that armaments are the only way to insure national security, then they will spend whatever it takes.

Another response those in the peace movement have made to military expenditures is to cite military waste. Outrageous examples, such as fifty-dollar screwdrivers that cost fifty cents at a hardware store, are thought to provide a good argument for reducing military spending. Such examples do not provide a good argument. In fact, such reasoning involves the fallacy of generalizing from unusual cases. It is no more proper to generalize about all military spending from a few odd examples than it is to generalize about all people on welfare from a few odd examples.

Targeting the waste in military spending is a trap for those interested in working for peace. Suppose that one points out an example of waste. So what? A person who holds the military view of defense will agree that waste should be eliminated. The military would like to get more weapons for their money. The issue for peace activists should not be the efficiency of the military, it should be the mission of the military and the need for that mission.

Those against military spending too often address themselves to limiting weapons without addressing the reason people feel they need weapons. People feel they need weapons because the other side has weapons. By arguing that one side should limit its weapons, those interested in peace appear to be helping the other side, or at least to be weakening their own country. In the military game, each side seeks to be better prepared for war than the other. Having on your side a peace movement dedicated to lowering your country's level of military preparedness is a minus. A peace movement is something you wish on your enemy.

Actions for peace involve questioning the necessity of waging war. Peace activists must make it clear that instead of taking sides within the existing climate of war they are attempting to abolish war. Peace activists oppose war not because they support the other side, but because they want a transformation to a world in which people settle their conflicts peacefully.

The emphasis on the question of whether to increase or decrease armaments assumes that the problem of achieving peace is a technical problem, with the amount of hardware providing the solution. Before World War II, the peace movement argued that nations should take steps towards disarmament to insure peace. That policy failed. Now nations assume that the way to peace is to have more and more armaments. That method also will fail because it makes the same false assumption that the previous policy made. Achieving peace involves establishing institutions that can keep the peace and motivating individuals to make those institutions work. It is not a technical problem that will be solved by having the right number of weapons.

The Task of Those Who Work for Peace

Those who work for peace must win over those who do not think that peace is possible. Their enemy is militarism—not the people in the military, but the military mentality that keeps everyone on one side or the other in inevitable violent conflict. For a peace movement to succeed, the military mentality must be replaced with an alternative.

Working for peace means presenting a peace alternative in which people act as planetary citizens seeking nonviolent resolution of conflicts. Many of the actions undertaken by peace activists do not communicate this alternative.

The best way to avoid traps while working for peace is to focus on alternatives to war. This might be done by strengthening international law and our global consciousness, so that international law is respected. Other steps outlined in this book include establishing ties between communities in the United States and the Soviet Union, educating for global consciousness, and establishing community peace centers. All of these are positive steps that threaten no one.

People who believe that peace is impossible have nothing to lose by letting us try. That they think it is impossible is no reason for them to stop people from trying. The approach I advocate does not attempt to remove the current security arrangements. It involves creating new arrangements that will make the old arrangements obsolete.

Peace activists must be careful that their activities really relate to peace, and they must make some effort to insure that their activities are perceived as being for peace. The job of peace activists is to provide an alternative to war and a motivation to accept that alternative.

2

■ ■ ■

Defining Peace

■ ■ ■

How we define peace determines how we work for peace. If our definition is too broad, we end up doing things that are not really related to peace; if it is too narrow, success at achieving our goals is not enough to bring peace. Either way we end up working hard and achieving nothing. Many things people do in the name of peace are not really related to its attainment. Our first step in working for peace, then, ought to be to define our goal.

Peace as Disarmament

Suppose that we were to achieve disarmament. Would that ensure that we no longer have to worry about war? Even if all the nuclear weapons in the world were destroyed, it would take only months for nations to rebuild their atomic arsenals. Nations have been disarmed only to rearm and go to war again. Even if all weapons were destroyed, the knowledge of how to make them would still be with us. We could build weapons again if we had an incentive to do so. The definition of peace as disarmament is too narrow because disarmament might be achieved without achieving peace.

Armaments are not the problem, but a symptom. The problem is that nations are insecure. If we can provide security by means other than national armaments, it would be easier to resolve the issue of removing weapons. Nations would no longer feel the same need for weapons, just as people in low crime areas do not feel the same need for weapons as those in high crime areas. Certainly disarmament is essential to human survival, but we must recognize that the issues of war and peace are much broader than the single issue of disarmament.

Peace as Removing All Conflicts

At a meeting of my community peace group, members took turns expressing their concerns regarding peace. Several people expressed their desire to learn to do away with personal anger. Others spoke of their need to love everyone and of their need to be at peace with themselves. People thought that all these factors related to the quest for world peace. I will argue that none of them relate directly to peace and that the definition of peace as the removal of all conflicts is too broad.

World peace does not involve peace with oneself, removing conflict, or doing away with anger. All kinds of conflicts exist within nations; yet, when intact, the institutions of the nation state succeed in preventing civil wars. One state in the United States does not go to war with another, despite economic conflicts between states and an abundance of power-hungry people.

It is easy to understand why people might think that peace requires loving one's neighbors, giving up all anger, or ending all conflicts. Certainly if we achieved these goals, we would achieve peace. However, it is a fallacy to think that peace requires the achievement of these goals. While it is true that "if there were no conflict, then there would be peace," we cannot infer from this statement that "if there is peace, then there is no conflict." And the same is true for "if we loved one another" and "if we had no anger." I know this because I know that there is peace between states in the United States—yet there are people who do not love each other, who have anger, and who have all kinds of conflicts with each other.

Those who seek world peace to avoid a nuclear catastrophe should seek the minimum necessary conditions for peace. It does not help to think of the most difficult ways of achieving peace. Many individuals I have met who claim to be devoting their lives to working for peace are actually working for personal ideals that have little to do with peace. These individuals actually hurt the cause of peace because they go about telling people that peace cannot be achieved without achieving much more difficult goals. They remind me of the people who would not help in the civil rights movement because they believed that socialism was necessary before civil rights could be achieved. The fact is that civil rights were achievable without socialism. And the fact is that peace is achievable without attaining the personal goals espoused by many so-called peace activists.

Kinds of Conflict We Are Concerned With

If we really believe that there is nothing more important than the prevention of war, then we should try to find the minimum conditions that are necessary for peace. While it is true that if we removed all conflicts, then there would be peace on earth, this is an impossible goal. The question we should ask is, "What kind of conflict does the person interested in working for peace have to be concerned with?"

Because there are various types of conflict, in defining peace, we must decide what types we are primarily concerned with, lest we dissipate our efforts. A list might include personal conflicts, family feuds, quarrels between communities, regions, races, religious and cultural groups, ideological conflicts, class conflicts, and conflicts between nations. If our primary concern is to prevent a nuclear holocaust, we are primarily concerned with conflicts between nations.

In addition to being concerned with conflicts between nations, we need to be concerned with civil wars and attacks on groups within nations. Civil wars are wars between groups that compete for sovereign power just as nations do. Attempts at subjugating or annihilating people who are of a different national, religious or ethnic group are also similar to nations making war against each other. These three types of conflict—conflicts between nations, conflicts between groups competing for national power, and actions against minorities within a nation—are all of interest to those concerned with human survival. The last two forms of conflict—civil wars and acts of war against minorities—can easily lead to wars between nations that support the opposing sides.

All conflicts have certain features in common, so the study of ways of settling domestic conflicts can have some bearing on the settling of international conflicts, but peace concerns mainly international conflicts. A person interested in working for peace should focus directly on conflicts between nations, with attention also to civil wars and the treatment of minorities within countries.

Removing, Reducing, and Resolving Conflicts

Having focused our attention on conflicts between nations, we must decide whether we are trying to remove, reduce, or resolve these conflicts. What has to happen to conflict for peace to exist? I will argue that those who believe that we must remove conflict, or even reduce conflict, are wrong. All that is necessary for peace to exist is that we have methods for resolving conflicts between nations.

Why would people believe that the removal of conflict is necessary for peace? We want a rational model of human behavior. On one side we have idealists who believe that people act from their sense of what is right and wrong. On the other side we have materialists who believe that people act from their interest in material gain. Both idealists and materialists believe that conflict has clear causes, and that peace requires the removal of those causes.

I call the idealist view of humanity "Homo rationalis." According to this view, humans are rational creatures who unfortunately cannot always agree on what is rational. This view is represented by Gottfried Wilhelm Leibniz, the seventeenth-century philosopher and mathematician, who believed that "most disputes arise from a lack of clarity in things, that is, from the failure to reduce them to numbers."[1] A pioneer in the development of symbolic logic, Leibniz dreamed of ending conflict by inventing a universal language to provide a method for determining what is rational. He explains how this would work in the area of religion. "Once missionaries are able to introduce this universal language, then also will the true religion, which stands in intimate harmony with reason, be established, and there will be as little reason to fear any apostasy in the future as to fear a renunciation of arithmetic and geometry once they have been learnt."[2]

I call the materialist view of humanity "Homo economis." According to this view human beings are creatures who are constantly calculating their individual and class economic interest. Karl Marx saw the solution to ending conflicts in doing away with class society, so that people would no longer have contrary economic interests.

Unfortunately, neither the idealist nor the materialist view leaves much room for irrational man, "Homo ludicrous." Homo ludicrous will get into a conflict over just about anything. Because Homo ludicrous is a numerous breed that will always be with us, it makes no sense to pin one's hopes for peace on ending conflict.

Human beings are simply not calculating machines, whether calculating either the merits of ideas or the advantages of actions in dollars. To find out what really motivates people we might examine advertising. Advertising experts have to know what motivates people—if their views are wrong, their products don't sell. What we learn from advertising is that although people like to think of themselves as rational, they are not. People are motivated by fear, hunger, sex, and rage, sometimes by a desire to do the right thing, and also sometimes by a desire to acquire possessions. All these factors play a role in conflict, and conflict, like these factors, will be with us forever.

The only requirement for peace is that we have a way to resolve conflicts between nations. We may want to achieve many other goals, such as to reduce the conflicts in the world, to work for social justice, and on and on. But it is not honest to claim that these other goals must be achieved for peace to be achieved. Certainly, reducing conflicts makes them easier to resolve. But reducing conflict and resolving conflict are two different things.

As personal goals I want to work for peace with myself, with the earth, and between people. There is a sense in which humanity is now at war with nature. I believe we must learn to live more simply and to do as little harm to this planet as we can, but it would be dishonest for me to claim that the way to work for peace is to work for all the things I advocate.

An Adequate Definition of Peace

Peace is primarily concerned with the nonviolent resolution of conflicts between nations, and, to a lesser extent, with the resolution of conflicts between groups vying for power within nations and the protection of minorities. It centers on conflicts between groups of people.

A person interested in working for peace should work to strengthen methods for resolving conflicts between nations and to foster an international consciousness so that those methods are used. As part of being concerned about other people, a person might be concerned with issues of justice, but peace is first and foremost concerned with getting nations to settle their differences without violence.

What is peace and when does it exist? Peace exists when there is a period of time during which there is no disposition towards fighting. Peace exists when nations are in the habit of resolving conflicts without violence. Peace exists when nations are able to and must resolve their conflicts without violence.

Three centuries ago, the English philosopher Thomas Hobbes observed that, "WAR, consisteth not in battle only, or the act of fighting; but in a tract of time, wherein the will to contend by battle is sufficiently known: and therefore the notion of *time,* is to be considered in the nature of war; as it is in the nature of weather. For as the nature of foul weather, lieth not in a shower or two of rain; but in an inclination thereto of many days together: so the nature of war, consisteth not in actual fighting; but in the known disposition thereto, during all the time there is no assurance to the contrary. All other time is PEACE."[3]

Are we at peace, or are we at war? We are told that this is peacetime, but preparations for war continue. Peace is usually thought of as the absence of open fighting, and war as open conflict. But I think that it is useful to use a broader definition of war and peace, and to speak of a climate of war and a climate of peace. Those interested in peace should start investigating positive steps that can be taken to create a climate of peace.

Peace exists when nations are in the habit of settling their conflicts without violence and are confident that violence will not be used. Given this definition, it is apparent that there is a difference between opposing a particular war and working for peace. There is also a difference between the negative action of criticizing the present notion of security through national armaments and taking positive steps to strengthen methods of nonviolent conflict resolution.

3

■ ■ ■

Resolving Conflicts
without Violence

■ ■ ■

Having defined peace as the nonviolent resolution of conflict between nations, the next questions are, How can conflicts between nations be resolved without violence? and What structures are necessary so that nations will develop the habit of settling their disputes without violence? In this chapter I argue that having an international authority provides a method for settling conflicts between nations.

Historical Evidence

Researchers interested in abolishing war look for different causes of war than those sought by historians. Historians explore the many motivations and interests of particular individuals. Researchers interested in preventing war look for what is common in instances where war occurs. To explain what brought events about, historians seek sufficient causes of those events. To understand how to prevent war, peace researchers seek the necessary conditions that must be present for war to occur.

Peace research must be a separate discipline, distinct from the history of diplomacy, because peace researchers ask different questions than those asked by historians. Historians focus on individual events or ask why particular individuals made the decisions they made. Peace researchers contrast areas in the world where there is peace with those where there is war and ask whether there is any factor that is present when there is peace that is lacking when there is war.

One study that asks questions relevant to the abolition of war is *The Anatomy of Peace* by Emery Reves. Reves claims that we can identify one factor that is present in all situations of peace that is lacking in all situations of war. According to him, the real cause of all wars has always been the same. In examining the cause of war Reves seeks a factor that is present when peace exists and is absent when there is war. He observes that "wars between groups of men forming social units always take place when these units—tribes, dynasties, churches, cities, nations—exercise unrestricted sovereign power" and that "wars between these social units cease the moment sovereign power is transferred from them to a larger or higher unit."[4]

From these observations Reves deduced what he called a social law: "War takes place whenever and wherever nonintegrated social units of equal sovereignty come into contact." He states that "wars always ceased when a higher unit established its own sovereignty, absorbing the sovereignties of the conflicting smaller social groups. After such transfers of sovereignty, a period of peace followed, which lasted only until the new social units came into contact. Then a new series of wars began."[5]

> The causes and reasons alleged by history to have brought about these conflicts are irrelevant, as they continued to exist long after the wars had ceased. Cities and provinces continue to compete with each other. Religious convictions are just as different today as they were during the religious wars.
>
> The only thing that did change was the institutionalization of sovereignty, the transfer of sovereignty from one type of social unit to another and a higher one.
>
> Just as there is one and only one cause for wars between men on this earth, so history shows that peace—not peace in an absolute and utopian sense, but concrete peace between given social groups warring with each other at given times—has always been established in one and only in one way.
>
> Peace between fighting groups of men was never possible and wars succeeded one another until some sovereignty, some sovereign source of law, some sovereign power was set up *over* and *above* the clashing social units, integrating the warring units into a higher sovereignty.[6]

Reves's claims can all be tested. Anyone can examine the evidence to decide whether these claims are correct. Considering the billions spent on weapons, the millions of people who die in war, and the threat of nuclear destruction, one might think that since 1945 many studies of these claims would have been made. But as Peter Rohn noted in 1976, "In international law we have not even reached the point where we take it for granted that a basic inventory of facts and magnitudes is both necessary and available."[7]

Empirical studies are rare. In "Conflict Resolution and the Structure of the State System," Gregory Raymond states that his method was "to recast traditional speculations into propositional form and confront these propositions with reproducible evidence." One proposition tested is the claim that "there is an inverse relationship between arbitral activity and the onset of war."[8] Raymond used a survey of international arbitral activity compiled by A.M. Stuyt that includes activity from the 1794 Jay Treaty to 1970 and correlated the use of arbitration with the incidence and magnitude of wars.[9] In his concluding chapter Raymond wrote, "As arbitration became more widely accepted as an important mode of conflict resolution, an upswing occurred in the number of states that used arbitration. Furthermore, as the scope of arbitral activity increased, the magnitude and severity of war decreased."[10]

Having warring nations become part of a larger political unit that has compulsory arbitration of disputes would prevent wars. In the case of international disputes, this would mean that nations would have to accept the rulings of an international court or would have to submit their disputes to binding arbitration. Raymond's study indicates that arbitration can prevent wars.

One can see how including warring parties in a larger political system prevents warfare by examining old fortresses. As one travels in Europe one sees castles. Why were castles needed and why did they become obsolete? They were needed because countries like Germany and Italy were once divided into many small sovereign states that waged war with each other. The fortresses became obsolete when these states became part of larger political units, and the state of war ended. From then on a common authority settled disputes between the people in the formerly warring states. People did not destroy the castles before being joined to a larger political unit. Their integration into a larger political unit made the castles obsolete.

We can test all the claims of Emery Reves by studying history and the relationship of the relevant factors, such as the use of arbitration and the incidence of war. What the evidence shows is that

the acceptance of a common judge (sovereign, arbiter, or authority) can replace war as a system for settling disputes.

The method of having two warring parties submit their disputes to a third party works. But why does it work? And is it the
only method that can work? Must people accept a system of arbitration? Can't they just reason together and settle their disputes
that way?

Theoretical Arguments for Accepting Authority

We can learn the conditions necessary for peace between nations
by examining the conditions necessary for peace within nations.
Seventeenth-century philosophers John Locke and Thomas Hobbes
both claimed that a common authority was a necessary condition
for peace within a state. I believe that their arguments for accepting a national authority apply to the acceptance of an international
authority. Locke argues in *The Second Treatise Of Government* that
when people do not have an authority to judge their conflicts, they
end up in a state of war.

> Men living together according to reason, without a common
> Superior on Earth, with Authority to judge between them, is *properly
> the State of Nature*. But force, or a declared design of force upon the
> Person of another, where there is no common Superior on Earth to
> appeal to for relief, *is the State of War:* And 'tis the want of such an
> appeal gives a Man the Right of War even against an *aggressor*,
> though he be in Society and a fellow Subject.[11]

It is interesting to note that Locke believes that people guided
only by reason end up at war with each other, and he argues for a
nonrational method of settling disputes—the acceptance of
authority. Thomas Hobbes shares Locke's view on the limits of
reason.

As I read Hobbes's *Leviathan*, Hobbes makes a distinction
between factual questions, which reason can settle, and non-factual
questions, which reason cannot settle. He believed that questions
of right and wrong, religion, and possession cannot be settled by
individuals reasoning together.[12] Since peace depends on settling
these questions, and they cannot be settled by reason, some other
method is needed. While we may differ on the necessity of settling
religious questions, all Hobbes needs for this argument is that we

grant that there are some disputes that reason cannot settle. I believe that Hobbes argues rationally for the acceptance of a non-rational method of settling the disputes that reason cannot settle. That method is the acceptance of authority.

What is authority? Above all else authority is a method of conflict resolution. Other words for "authority" in this context are "arbiter," "representative," and "sovereign." Hobbes explains how this method of conflict resolution works. "A multitude of men, are made *one* person, when they are by one man, or one person, represented; so that it be done with the consent of every one of that multitude in particular. For it is the *unity* of representer, not the *unity* of the represented, that maketh the person *one*. And it is the representer that beareth the person, and but one person: and *unity*, cannot otherwise be understood in multitude."[13]

The institution of authority replaces the reason of many with the reason of one. Hobbes speaks of the difference between the reasoning of private individuals and the reason of an authority. "It is not that *juris prudentia*, or wisdom of subordinate judges; but the reason of this our artificial man the commonwealth, and his command, that maketh law: and the commonwealth being in their representative but one person, there cannot easily arise any contradiction in the laws; and when there doth, the same reason is able, by interpretation, or alteration, to take it away."[14]

Here, then, is a method for removing contradictions of interests and viewpoints by having the conflicting parties accept the judgment of a third party. The representative they accept represents both; yet, because the arbiter is one person, the arbiter speaks with one voice. The arbiter represents them in that he or she acts for them, and they give up their ability to act. This method resolves conflicts by creating a situation in which the formerly disputing parties can no longer express their conflicting views.

Locke also argues for the acceptance of a national authority as a method for settling conflicts.

> To avoid this State of War (wherein there is no appeal but to Heaven, and wherein every the least difference is apt to end, where there is no Authority to decide between the Contenders) is one great *reason of Mens putting themselves into Society,* and quitting the State of Nature. For where there is an Authority, a Power on Earth, from which relief can be had by *appeal*, there the continuance of the State of War is excluded, and the Controversie is settled by that Power.[15]

An authority provides a way to settle conflicts. A person seeking an end to civil war does not have to remove the causes of conflict. According to both Hobbes and Locke, there will always be conflicts that reason cannot resolve. People need only a method for resolving these conflicts.

Argument for Accepting an International Authority

The solution to conflict is to prevent conflict from leading to violence. The solution to war is to prevent people from fighting wars. Just as we can prevent violence between individuals by not allowing individuals to settle their conflicts by the use of force, we could prevent violence between nations by not allowing nations to settle their conflicts by the use of force.

What is the cause of war and what is the cure? According to Emery Reves wars occur when sovereign nations challenge each other, and wars do not occur when formerly warring parties are incorporated into a larger political unit. Why is this? It is because the larger political unit will not allow warfare and insists that the parties that had formerly been at war submit to a common authority to settle their disputes. The state of war ends between formerly warring parties when they can no longer wage war and must instead submit their disputes to an arbiter.

In examining the cause of war and the cure I will relate an experience that I believe is instructive. I was in a restaurant when a couple came in with a little boy. The little boy got up from the table where the couple was seated, left his plate of food, and walked around the restaurant staring at and even asking for other people's food. The couple did nothing. My question is, What was the cause of the boy's behavior? Was it the child's curiosity, his hunger, or his not liking his own food? Didn't he behave that way because his parents did not stop him? Why do we have wars? We have wars because nations are allowed to wage war—because no one stops nations from waging war.

What is the lesson from historical experience and theory? Historical experience shows that when nations are no longer allowed to wage war because they are incorporated into a larger political unit, war ceases. Experience shows that when nations are forced to accept the verdict of an arbiter and not allowed to settle their disputes with force, war ceases. Theory shows that reason has limits and the acceptance of an authority system is sometimes the only way to settle disputes. Arbitration settles disputes by having two parties accept the judgment of a third party. If we established an international authority and enforced international law we would abolish war.

What would an international authority be able to accomplish? Nations with conflicts would have someplace to go to settle their disputes peacefully. An international authority might handle disputes between nations and not get involved in civil disputes. Should nations accept an international authority, as citizens accept national authorities, then disputes between nations would be settled without violence.

Can it work? It does work. The use of a judge, arbiter, or authority has been the main method of conflict resolution used throughout history. The fact that every day there is peace among the respective communities and regions of nations demonstrates its efficacy. We do not need years of studies in conflict resolution to know that having an international authority would provide a method of settling international conflicts.

Part II

Outlawing War

From *My Fellow Americans* by Ron Cobb, with permission of Price/Stern/Sloan, Inc., Los Angeles.

■ For I dipt into the future, far as human eye
   can see,
   See the Vision of the world, and all the
     wonder that would be;
   Till the war-drum throbb'd no longer, and the
     battle flags all furl'd
   In the Parliament of man, the Federation of
     the world.

—Alfred Lord Tennyson

4

■■■

The Alternative to War

■■■

War cannot be abolished until alternative institutions exist to provide for the nonviolent settling of disputes. Fortunately, institutions have been designed in the past and are being designed in the present for the purpose of eliminating war. The writers of the U.S. Constitution consciously sought to create an institution that would abolish war in the new world. With the exception of the Civil War, this institution has worked. Today, the European Community is attempting to abolish war in Europe. The founding of the United States and the founding of the European Community provide two different models of how we might abolish war.

Institutions Needed to Replace War

War is an institution that human beings invented. Not all people have had the institution of war. Eskimos were unfamiliar with the institution. Because not all people have the institution of war, the anthropologist Margaret Mead observed that "warfare is only an invention—not a biological necessity."[1] Nor is war a necessity based on level of development. Some people at the same level of development as Eskimos have war, and others do not. Mead wrote that "simple peoples and civilized peoples, mild peoples and violent assertive peoples, will all go to war if they have the invention, just as those peoples who have the custom of dueling will have duels and people who have the pattern of vendetta will indulge in vendetta" (p. 115). How can people who have the institution of war relinquish this institution? According to Mead:

For this, two conditions at least are necessary. The people must recognize the defects of the old invention, and someone must make a new one. Propaganda against warfare, documentation of its terrible cost in human suffering and social waste, these prepare the ground by teaching people to feel that warfare is a defective social institution. There is further needed a belief that social invention is possible and the invention of new methods which will render warfare as out-of-date as the tractor is making the plow, or the motor car the horse and buggy. A form of behavior becomes out-of-date only when something else takes its place, and in order to invent forms of behavior which will make war obsolete, it is a first requirement to believe that an invention is possible. (pp. 117–18)

The faults of the institution of war are apparent to all today. We could annihilate ourselves with nuclear weapons. The peace movement has pointed out the problems with the war system, but who is working on building the institutions that can replace war? What is the alternative to war?

The alternative to war is law. Using politics within a system of government, a system of law settles the conflicts previously settled by war. We know that this can work. It works on the level of the small community, the city, the state, and the nation. In each case it usually allows us to control conflicts between the groups under its jurisdiction. Sometimes law doesn't work and conflicts are not contained, such as with the Civil War in the United States or the current ethnic conflicts in the Soviet Union. But for the most part, politics within a system of government provides a method of containing conflict.

If, as Karl von Clausewitz states "war is the carrying out of political aims by violent means,"[2] then the abolition of war must make possible the carrying out of political aims by nonviolent means. Those who would abolish war must build institutions that provide people a nonviolent means of seeking goals that are usually sought through war. This nonviolent means can be accomplished by having formerly warring parties within a system of government.

Given that the alternative to war is some system of government, it is apparent that the alternative to war between nations is an international system of government for handling the conflicts between nations. Peace activists should direct their attention to building legislative and judicial systems that can resolve international disputes.

War today fails to accomplish what it once could. War was the means by which one nation was able to impose its will on another. The waging of war served the same function on an international level that submitting disputes to an arbiter might serve. In both cases it was possible to get a definite result. Today, because of nuclear weapons, the world community cannot allow one side to use all its force against another. The nuclear nations cannot engage in war against each other, and they will not allow other nations to engage in total war for fear that they will become involved. One strange result is that although Israel has "won" five wars against Arab nations, those wars settled nothing. In previous times the victorious nation would have destroyed its enemies.

While war cannot be used as the arbiter of international disputes, at present nothing else exists that can be used, there is no binding authority that can be appealed to. Peace activists are often impatient with the leaders of the world's nations. They ask, Why don't the leaders see that war is obsolete? War is not obsolete. War won't be obsolete until we replace it with another method of resolving conflicts. The job of those interested in peace is not to chastise national leaders for not acknowledging that war is obsolete, but to make war obsolete by producing an alternative.

The U.S. Constitution

The founders of the United States consciously sought to create institutions that would abolish war in the new world. The institutions they created made war between states obsolete. With the exception of the Civil War, the Constitution has served states as a means of settling disputes with each other, and it can provide a model for uniting all the states of the world.

Between 1783, when a treaty was signed with England, and 1789, when the Constitution was ratified, thirteen separate nations occupied the area of the United States, in addition to colonies of Spain, England, and France. The thirteen former colonies of England were no more united than are nations of the United Nations. Indeed the Articles of Confederation that united the thirteen colonies in many ways parallels the United Nations. The Articles of Confederation had no independent taxing powers, no judiciary, and no power to enforce laws, all weaknesses of the United Nations today.

The separate nations that made up the Articles of Confederation were in danger of waging war against each other. New York and New Jersey had a battle over the question of who could tax incoming ships. Connecticut and Massachusetts fought over the acquisition of land to their west. An armed taxpayers' revolt, Shay's Rebellion, occurred in Massachusetts. England kept a chain of forts within the territory of the colonies and Spain controlled navigation on the Mississippi River.[3]

These nations differed in their economic interests, customs, and, in some cases, language. Pennsylvania wanted to make German its national tongue, for most of its inhabitants spoke German and not English. The colonies were not unified in either culture or even proximity. From South Carolina it was as easy to go to England as to Boston.[4] Although threatened by the bordering English, French, and Spanish colonies and by Indian raids, funds for the common army of 750 were impossible to raise by direct taxation. The confederation was dependent on voluntary contributions from the states and of the $10 million requisitioned by Congress only $1.5 million was paid, with one state paying nothing at all.[5]

The division between former colonies prompted Josiah Tucker, a contemporary liberal philosopher, to predict in 1786 that "the mutual antipathies and clashing interests of the Americans, their differences of governments, habitudes, and manners, indicate that they will have no centre of union and no common interest. They never can be united into one compact empire under any species of government whatever; a disunited people till the end of time, suspicious and distrustful of each other, they will be divided and subdivided into little commonwealths or principalities."[6]

A few far-sighted leaders sought to unite the former colonies in a way that would abolish war between them. They saw the need to strengthen the Articles of Confederation and persuaded the Continental Congress to call a convention in Philadelphia in May 1787 to reform the Articles of Confederation. Those who attended wrote a new constitution, so now we call it the Constitutional Convention.

Seventy-four delegates were selected from the thirteen states, but only fifty-five showed up from time to time. Rhode Island did not even bother to send anyone. After one month of wrangling, the delegates present decided it would be impossible to reform the Articles of Confederation, so they locked the doors, kept out the press, and sat down to draw up a new form of government. George

Washington said in a speech to the convention, "It is too probable that no plan we propose will be adopted. Perhaps another dreadful conflict is to be sustained. If, to please the people, we offer what we ourselves disapprove, how can we afterward defend our work? Let us raise a standard to which the wise and honest can repair."[7]

In a month the convention became stalemated on the question of representation in Congress. The big states led by Edmund Randolph of Virginia wanted proportional representation based on population, whereas the little states led by William Paterson of New Jersey wanted equal representation for each state. Washington was ready to give up and go home when at the last moment, a delegate from Connecticut named Roger Sherman came up with the Great Compromise that saved the convention. He suggested that one house of Congress have equal representation to satisfy and protect the small states and a second house have representation based upon population to satisfy and protect the big states. The delegates accepted this compromise.

The form of government worked out was a federal system, in which a constitution divides governmental powers between the central government and the states, in contrast with a unitary system, in which the central government determines the power of local units. The constitution in a federal system establishes the power of both the central and the local governments. Each unit of government has power that is independent of the wishes of those at other levels of government. The Constitution of the United States specifies the powers of the national government and reserves to the states powers not granted the national government.

The founders worked out the checks and balances that have made this government so workable. They feared the possibility of a king emerging, so they made sure this could not happen. The three branches of government—the legislative, executive, and judicial—check and balance each other.

The uniting of thirteen separate nations into one by the consent of the governed was an unparalleled feat. George Washington wrote to Lafayette on February 7, 1788, "It appears to me, then, little short of a miracle, that the Delegates from so many different states (which states you know are also different from each other), in their manner, circumstances, and prejudices, should unite in forming a system of national government, so little liable to well founded objections."[8]

The U.S. Constitution combined thirteen separate nations

into one larger unit for the purpose of preventing war between the separate nation states. Debates would continue concerning the nature of that union. Some would argue that the Constitution combined these nation states and reserved all rights to these states that were not expressly given to the national government, the states' rights view. Others would say that the sovereignty rested not in the nation states but in the people of the states, who had the ability to give the nation more and more powers.

When George Washington led his army against the English, the colonists viewed themselves as members of their individual states and had little loyalty to a larger unit. Even up to the Civil War many individuals viewed themselves as first and foremost citizens of their states. The issue of whether one is a citizen of one's state first or a citizen of the United States was played out (with racist overtones) in the civil rights struggle of the 1960s. Behind such struggles lies the issue of whether the state or the national government is sovereign, or whether individuals always retain sovereignty.

One of the biggest obstacles faced by the founding fathers was the issue of limiting the sovereignty of states so that those states might become part of a larger political unit. William Paterson of New Jersey raised an issue of concern to many delegates: "We are met here as the deputies of thirteen independent, sovereign states, for federal purpose. Can we consolidate their sovereignty and form one nation, and annihilate the sovereignties of our states who have sent us here for our purposes?" James Wilson of Pennsylvania understood that the issue was one of each state giving up part of its sovereignty when he replied, "The gentleman from New Jersey is candid in declaring his opinion. I commend him for it. I am equally so. I say again I never will confederate on his principles. If no state will part with any of its sovereignty it is vain to talk of a national government."[9]

Someday the world may look on the United Nations as we look on the Articles of Confederation. Individuals in the movement to abolish war are asking nations to either reform the United Nations or to form a stronger organization. Some argue that individuals have the right to by-pass their national governments if nations do not act, because the people retain sovereign power and can transfer part of their sovereignty to a world government.

The argument is often made that the states of the United States had more in common than the nations of the world today.

The evidence is ambiguous. Today the nations of the world are more integrated and interdependent than the thirteen colonies were. Whereas it took them weeks to communicate, today we have instantaneous communications. We can travel from one end of the globe to another more quickly than they could travel from one end of the colonies to the other. Modern commerce has connected the nations of the world more tightly than the self-sufficient colonies were tied to each other. Finally, nations today are more conscious of a common fate because all are in thrall to the worldwide ecological crisis and the threat of atomic warfare.

The writers of the Constitution were aware that they had devised a method for abolishing war in the new world and they thought their method could be applied to abolish war in Europe. One month after the convention adjourned, Benjamin Franklin sent a copy of the proposed Constitution to a friend in France with this note: "If it succeeds, I do not see why you might not in Europe carry the project of good Henry the Fourth into execution, by forming a Federal Union and One Grand Republic of all its different States and Kingdoms, by means of a like Convention; for we had many interests to reconcile."[10]

The convention delegates were interested in researching the causes of war in order to seek its abolition. At the convention James Madison stated, "The same causes which have rendered the old world the Theater of incessant wars, and have banished liberty from the face of it, would soon produce the same effects here."[11] Madison and Alexander Hamilton devoted an entire issue of *The Federalist* to examining the experiences of the weak confederations of ancient Greek republics, asking whether the cause of war between these states was their experimentation with democracy. They concluded that war was caused by unrestrained sovereignty, not democracy, and the cure was to form a larger political unit.

The founders thought they were providing a model for both the abolition of war and the preservation of liberty. A Massachusetts delegate, Elbridge Gerry, called himself a "representative of the whole human race" and declared that "something must be done, or we shall disappoint not only America, but the whole world."[12]

To seek a way out of our predicament today, it is fitting that we examine how the thirteen colonies were able to abolish war among themselves. The parallels are many between the situation we find ourselves in today and the situation of the colonies. The Articles of Confederation set up a loose, ineffective confederation of sovereign states, and so does the United Nations. The founders of the United States decided to end the anarchy between the states, and people today can end the anarchy in international affairs.

Just as some people say that nations today will never accept imposed international law, many said that the thirteen colonies would never be able to unite. Getting the Constitution ratified was difficult. Only thirty-eight of the fifty-five delegates would sign it, and seventeen went back to their states to lobby against ratification. During the first year eleven states ratified. Then it passed in New Hampshire by seventeen votes, in Virginia by ten votes, and in New York, by only three votes. North Carolina wavered, rejecting it and then ratifying it. Rhode Island held out until 1790 when it ratified it by a two-vote margin.

Agreement wasn't easy then, and it won't be easy now, although today, in addition to the example of the United States, we have the example of the European Community.

The European Community

The movement for a united Europe got its greatest impetus when Winston Churchill called for a United States of Europe in 1946.[13] His call offered hope amid the devastation of war. The next step came in 1950, when the French minister of foreign affairs, Robert Schuman, proposed that European nations set up an organization to pool the production and consumption of coal and steel. This organization, the European Coal and Steel Community (ECSC), was the first experiment in European federation. As established by a 1951 treaty in Paris, the ECSC was given a council of ministers, a court of justice, and a parliamentary assembly. Its first members included France, the Federal Republic of Germany, Italy, Belgium, the Netherlands, and Luxembourg.

Following the success of the ECSC, the European Economic Community (EEC), and the European Atomic Energy Community (Euratom) were established. Treaties signed in Rome in 1958 called for the political union of the peoples of Europe. While each of the three communities had separate executive commissions, a common parliament and court were established, with members of the first parliament appointed by national parliaments and are subsequently elected. These institutions constitute the European Community.

The immediate objective of the European Community is the

removal of all quotas and barriers to trade. Once implemented, it will allow free movement of persons, goods, services, and capital. The European Community's economic progress made membership attractive, and Greece and Turkey became members in 1959.

In 1961, progress was made toward political union when member states agreed to hold regular meetings for political consultation. In the same year, Ireland, Denmark, and the United Kingdom submitted applications for membership. Also in 1961, the six original members and a large number of African countries held a meeting in Brussels, the first step in a continuing relationship between the European Community and the developing nations. In 1973, the United Kingdom, Ireland, and Denmark joined the European Community.

In June 1979, over a hundred million Europeans went to the polls to elect representatives to the European Parliament, which can pass laws directly binding on the member nations, and in some cases directly binding on the individuals living in member countries.

On April 18, 1990, at a meeting in Dublin, the leaders of the European Community adopted a plan to achieve political union by January 1993, a speedy merger spurred in part by the speed of German unification. Many issues—insuring that a united Germany does not threaten peace, the role of NATO and the Warsaw Pact, the independence of the Baltic States from the Soviet Union—must now be seen in the context of the emerging European Community.

Two Models for the Abolition of War

The U.S. Constitution and the European Community provide contrasting models of ways to abolish war, and our choice of actions in abolishing war worldwide is determined in part by the model we follow.

The differences between the federal government model of the United States and the community of nations model of the European Community can be illustrated by considering what would happen if nations worldwide followed each model. Following the federal government model, nation states would establish an international organization as a central government that is limited in function, with current nation states reserving for themselves powers not given to the central government. In the community model, nations would give up their sovereignty in specific areas to specific authorities that would not constitute a new government. One authority might control international air travel and another, disarmament. In addition to being another model for an alternative to war the community of nations model is another model for national sovereignty.

The European union is called a community, which contrasts it with a government that is unitary, international, supranational, or federal. Each nation gives up a well-defined part of its national sovereignty to the community, which is competent in certain limited spheres established by treaties. This contrasts with setting up a unitary government that could intervene in local areas. It is more than an international treaty between sovereign states, but less than a government above the existing governments. The founders of the European Community rejected the term "federal" because some felt that it implied that they were establishing a government rather than authorities in specific areas. The community is, of course, a federal model in that powers are clearly limited.

The community model provides us with another alternative solution to problems that involve war and sovereignty. By redefining the ideas of nation state and sovereignty, it allows us to think of solutions to problems that might not otherwise be solvable. The desire of Palestinians for their own state and Israel's need for security might both be accommodated by a federated community that includes Israel, Palestine, and Jordan. Abba Eban, a former foreign minister of Israel, suggests a federation that would share a common market.[14] Sovereignty could be redefined so that no member of the federation could wage war against another.

It is entirely possible that the Soviet Union will evolve into a federation similar to the European Community. This federation might expand by a voluntary process to embrace many of the nations of Eastern Europe and eventually merge with the European Community.

We have two models of how a world federation might occur. Following the U.S. model we could convene a conference to either reform the United Nations or replace it with a more powerful organization. Following the European model we might set up international institutions in limited areas, such as a court to try airplane terrorists. These models show us actions we can take to create either an international authority or international authorities.

5

■ ■ ■

Organizations Working
to Outlaw War

■ ■ ■

Organizations working to outlaw war differ according to their views of how the desired change might come about. Some organizations believe that the United Nations as constituted is the best hope for peace and try to show their support for it. The United Nations Association publicizes the work of the UN and builds support for UN funding. Other organizations try to reform the United Nations so that it might be able to enforce international law. The World Federalist Association serves this purpose with its Campaign for UN Reform, while it is also open to the possibility of forming a stronger world organization. The American Movement for World Government, like the World Federalists, wants either to strengthen the United Nations or replace it with a stronger organization; unlike the World Federalists they believe in openly advocating world government. The World Constitution and Parliament Association has given up on the United Nations and has its own constitution to establish a World Parliament. The World Association of World Citizens believes that the effort for world government begins with individuals renouncing their national citizenship and viewing themselves as world citizens.

While the various groups differ on methods for outlawing war they are not usually in conflict. No one knows what method will work, so most advocates of world peace through world law are willing to try different methods. Some individuals are members of several organizations. Tom A. Hudgens, a retired airline captain, has served as president of the Colorado chapter of the World Federalist Association, as vice-president of the American Movement for World Government, and as treasurer of the World Constitution and Parliament Association.

The United Nations

The United Nations has successes every day in providing vaccinations, improving diets in poor nations, and hundreds of other activities that it conducts through more than 150 agencies and centers. However, when most people discuss whether the UN is a success they have in mind larger accomplishments. Prior to the Persian Gulf War, the United Nations had enjoyed a string of successes. The UN mediated an end to the war between Iran and Iraq. UN Secretary-General Javier Pérez de Cuéllar helped Afghanistan, the Soviet Union, Pakistan, and the United States negotiate the Soviet withdrawal from Afghanistan. UN sanctions against South Africa helped start the process of change in that nation, and the UN helped Namibia gain independence. It mediated cease-fires between Angola and Namibia and between the factions fighting in Cambodia.

The UN's response to Iraq's August 2, 1990, invasion of Kuwait showed that it can stop aggression. First, UN resolutions established an embargo so that Iraq could not export oil or import anything other than food and medicine. On November 29, the UN passed a resolution authorizing its members to use "all necessary force" after January 15, 1991, to make Iraq implement previous UN resolutions calling for an end to the occupation of Kuwait. On January 17, the Persian Gulf War began, ending on February 28 when Iraq agreed to comply with all twelve relevant UN resolutions.

It is, of course, better to prevent an aggression than to have to end one. Most people are not aware of all the important disputes that the United Nations has helped to settle, such as the dispute between Iran and Bahrain. Iran claimed that when the British mandate ended in 1971, Bahrain should be part of Iran because historically Bahrain had been part of Iran. UN Secretary-General U Thant appointed a special commissioner who concluded that the islands' inhabitants wanted a fully independent sovereign state, and the Shah of Iran backed down on his claim. Were it not for the United Nations, Iran might have invaded Bahrain just as Iraq invaded Kuwait.

The UN Charter included provisions for a permanent military

force, but the UN has used peacekeeping forces on an ad hoc basis. After the Korean War, which was supported by the UN but fought mostly by U.S. forces, the UN chose to rely on the armed forces of small, neutral countries. These peacekeeping forces have been useful in separating warring parties and facilitating negotiated settlements. UN forces monitored the disengagement of Egyptian and Israeli armies in 1973 and supervised a buffer zone between the combatants until the Camp David Accords ended hostilities between Egypt and Israel. Since 1974 a UN Disengagement Observer Force has watched over the Golan Heights to limit forces and armaments between Israel and Syria. In Cyprus, UN forces have provided a buffer zone between the Greek and Turkish population since 1964. In 1978, the UN Interim Force in Lebanon was established to monitor the withdrawal of Israeli forces and help the government of Lebanon reestablish its authority. In 1988, when the UN sent 350 military observers to monitor a cease-fire between Iran and Iraq and fifty observers to monitor the Soviet withdrawal from Afghanistan, UN peacekeeping forces received the Nobel Peace Prize. In 1989 the UN deployed a force to oversee Namibia's transition to independence. All of these activities, with the exception of those in Lebanon, served to save lives.

The United Nations Association–USA

The main role of any United Nations Association is to inform the public about the United Nations. These associations, which exist in over sixty countries, are members of a World Federation of United Nations Associations established by a 1946 UN resolution that states, "The United Nations cannot achieve the purposes for which it has been created unless the peoples of the world are fully informed of its aims and activities."

The United Nations Association of the United States leads celebrations of the UN's birthday, October 24, preparing information kits for community UN day programs. Schools or regions who sponsor the Model UN program, a popular activity with young people who are able to act as UN representatives, receive from the association resource materials on writing background papers and running Model United Nations Conferences on particular issues. The association's "Mutilateral Project," which reexamines global issues in yearly reports, is currently examining chronic hunger, international cooperation in space, keeping the peace, and U.S.

policy toward the United Nations. The United Nations Association is active in urging members of Congress to support full funding for the UN.

In 1990, the United States owed the United Nations over $500 million. At the same time that the United States was urging the UN to do more—in the Persian Gulf, in Nicaragua to demobilize the Contras, in Cambodia to end their civil war—we have fallen behind in paying our assessed share of 25 percent of the UN budget, set according to our national income. The United States had refused to pay its share because of purported inefficiency and bias against this country in the UN. The United Nations answered the charge of inefficiency by firing 15 percent of its staff and the charge of bias by changing the leadership of UNESCO. Still the United States did not pay its dues, because the problem of paying dues had gotten caught up in the general budget deficit. Of the $216 million for current dues and $40 million for arrears that President Bush asked for, Congress voted only $130 million. Funding for the UN simply has not had the support that funding for other programs has had. One task of the United Nations Association–USA, and of the World Federalist Association described below, is to build a constituency to support full funding for the United Nations.

World Federalism

After World War II, people in many places wanted to put an end to war. The World Federalist movement, the Union of European Federalists, and the United World Federalists were all founded in 1947, the first two one week apart at congresses at Montreux,[15] and the latter in Asheville, North Carolina.

By 1986 the Union of European Federalists had attained a membership of 50,000 and the ability to mount demonstrations of up to 100,000 participants.[16] Federalists in Europe have thought in terms of incremental steps consistent with the development of the European Community and have been active in winning support for the development of that community.

The United World Federalists in the United States peaked in 1949 at over 40,000 members, with twenty full time staff members. Membership declined with the 1950 North Korean attack on South Korea when the United States found itself doing most of the fighting for UN forces engaged against an enemy supported by the

Soviet Union and China. Many members lost hope that Communist nations would support enforced international law. Meanwhile, propagandists of the far right attacked world government and the United World Federalists as communist-inspired. While the United World Federalists was not a major target of Sen. Joseph McCarthy— he was busy claiming that there were Communists in government— the attacks on people who did not conform created a climate in which people were reluctant to join organizations.

The United World Federalists changed its name to World Federalist United States of America in 1969 and became primarily a lobbying organization. A new sense of professionalism came with the lobbying function and professionals and volunteers did not work well together. Because of staff problems, personality clashes, the general paranoia of the times, and the failure of their lobbying efforts, WF-USA membership dwindled.

In 1975, the national executive board of WF-USA decided to merge with New Directions, a multi-issue group that claimed many famous adherents, including Margaret Mead, and had world federalism as one of its issues. Although the majority of the board of WF-USA voted to cease separate existence and to turn all assets over to New Directions, a small group of board members feared the end of the world federalist political movement and formed separate lobbying and electioneering committees that later merged into the Campaign for UN Reform. Their fears proved well-founded when New Directions later folded.

As a political action group, the Campaign for UN Reform does not have tax advantages. From it grew the tax-exempt World Federalist Education Fund, which became the World Federalist Association, and the membership of WF-USA was transferred to the new association.

The world federalist movement received new impetus when the Campaign for UN Reform started claiming some victories. In 1977, members of the board of directors were able to get Senators George McGovern and Howard Baker to cosponsor legislation tacked onto an appropriations bill that mandated Congress to address weaknesses in the United Nations and to report on recommendations for improvement. Since 1975, membership in the movement has grown to 8,000 members, and the number of chapters has grown to more than sixty.

The lessons from its past show that the two strengths of the world federalist movement are the specificity of its aim and its ability to influence Congress. Joining with a multi-issue organization, New Directions, was almost fatal. Having only one cause—world peace through world law—is a strength. The past shows also the importance of claiming some victories. Some of the campaign's successes have been out of proportion to its membership—it has written legislation that passed in Congress.

The Campaign for UN Reform supports measures to strengthen the United Nations, rates political candidates on whether they support these and other measures, and works for the election of candidates who favor them. The measures include expanding the jurisdiction of the International Court of Justice, improving the peacekeeping capacity of the United Nations with a standing army and reserves made up of designated national contingents, and changing the rules that allow one nation to veto the use of peacekeeping forces. Reformers want to improve the voting system in the UN General Assembly by taking into account both the population of countries and their financial contributions to the United Nations. The campaign would create an international criminal court to try those who violate international laws, such as hijackers, and create more effective methods of protecting human rights with a high commissioner appointed to investigate violations. The campaign is also working to set up an international disarmament agency to provide for verification of arms control agreements and to develop firm guidelines for protecting the environment with means to enforce regulations.

Parliamentarians for World Order, organized in 1978 by six national groups of parliamentarians, was originally affiliated with the World Federalist Movement. Now called Parliamentarians' Global Action, this group has more than six hundred members in twenty-four countries.

American Movement for World Government

The American Movement for World Government came into existence during the decline of the United World Federalists in the 1950s. Several members of UWF quit that organization because they felt that it had given up the advocacy of world government. The AMWG uses the phrase "world government" openly, because, as member Bill Cox said in a talk at the WorldView '84 Conference in Washington, D.C., "What you're really talking about is world government."

According to members of the World Federalist Association, it's not a simple case of being either for or against world government. From an editorial in the *World Federalist:* "It is not necessary or even desirable for nations to give up 'their sovereignty.' What is necessary is for them to give up that minor part of their sovereignty that permits them to make war, to injure other nations in other ways, and to prevent united global action in dealing with intractable global problems."[17]

The AMWG, which is trying to put together a World Constitutional Convention, draws a parallel between the United Nations and the Articles of Confederation. Just as the founders of the United States found that it was easier to write a new constitution than to reform the Articles, the AMWG wants to replace a United Nations flawed by major powers' veto power over its actions with another world body.

World Constitution and Parliament Association

Members of the World Constitution and Parliament Association are not waiting for the world's politicians to outlaw war. Their World Constituent Assembly in Innsbruck, Austria, in 1977 adopted a Constitution for the Federation of the Earth, which includes a diagram of world government. The WCPA has formed a parliament and seeks ratification of the constitution and implementation of such legislation as World Legislative Bill #1, the purpose of which is "to outlaw nuclear weapons and other weapons of mass destruction, and to establish a World Disarmament Agency which will be created and empowered by those who ratify the world legislation." One way to become a member of the provisional world parliament is by securing five hundred signatures on election petitions.

The WCPA's parliamentary working commissions deal with such issues as world economic development, global environmental protection, world population problems, and ownership of oceans. An Earth Rescue Corps consists of teams that will travel around the world to as many countries as possible to obtain ratification and implementation of urgent world legislation.

World Association of World Citizens

World citizens are not waiting until the Constitution of the Federation of Earth is ratified. They have already declared themselves world citizens, among them, Gary Davis, who in 1948 announced that he was a world citizen and not subject to the laws of any nation. Davis urged others to join him. The World Association of World Citizens keeps an international registry of world citizens, who are invited to attend its assemblies, held once every three years.

One way to test the effectiveness of a way of working for peace is to ask whether achieving the organization's goals would be sufficient for achieving peace and whether peace could be achieved without achieving those goals. Suppose all people called themselves world citizens? Would that bring peace about? I don't think so. Must everyone no longer be an American, a Russian, and so forth, for there to be peace? Must world citizen be our only identity?

I don't think that we need to give up any of our identities—we just have to add one. We can be, for instance, Americans *and* citizens of the world. Under the federalist model, local decisions would still be made on a local level, national decisions regarding national economies would be made on a national level, and all that would be changed is that there would be a new, international level added. International disputes would have to be settled on the international level.

Progress toward Outlawing War

Most people don't want to spend time working in organizations unless they think the organization has a chance of achieving its goals. Recent developments in the peace movement, the United Nations, and the U.S. Congress show that progress can be made toward outlawing war.

One of the largest peace organizations in the United States is now working to strengthen the United Nations. Two organizations, the Committee for a Sane Nuclear Policy (SANE) and the Nuclear Weapons Freeze Campaign, merged in 1987 to form SANE/FREEZE: Campaign for Global Security. The statement of purpose of this 177,000-member organization says, "We will work to see that the United States becomes a leader in efforts to eliminate war and the roots of violent conflict, including working to strengthen the United Nations and other international organizations."

The emphasis on strengthening the UN is new for both groups. Although SANE's cofounder was Norman Cousins, then president of the World Federalist Association, its activities over the past thirty years have been confined to opposing nuclear weapons testing, the Vietnam war, ABM systems, the MX missile, and other weapons. The Nuclear Weapons Freeze Campaign was founded in 1981 to stop the development of new weapons systems. Through its Freeze Voter affiliate, this group coordinated campaigns to support congressional freeze resolutions. The 1984 landslide victory of Ronald Reagan convinced peace movement leaders that a nuclear freeze was not an attainable goal. Recognizing that nations would be more likely to abolish weapons if they had another system of security, they began to advocate strengthening international institutions for peacekeeping, including the United Nations and the World Court.

In 1989 the peace movement came together for a Structures for Peace Conference organized by the World Federalist Association and co-sponsored by over a hundred organizations, including SANE/FREEZE, the United Nations Association, the Better World Society, and the American Association of University Women. The main theme was Common Security through Structures for Peace with discussion focusing on ways to strengthen the United Nations. Participants at the February gathering agreed to establish a Unity Process Committee to facilitate greater coordination in the peace movement. Walter Hoffmann, executive director of the World Federalist Association, and Sarah Harder, president of the American Association of University Women, were elected co-chairs of the committee. The first meeting was hosted in May 1989 by the National Peace Institute Foundation, the organization that had led the successful campaign to establish the U.S. Institute of Peace.

In April 1990 many of the organizations that co-sponsored the Structures for Peace Conference formed the Alliance for Our Common Future to cooperate on selected issues.[18] They formed a task force on the United Nations and decided to begin a campaign for full UN funding by Congress.[19]

Through efforts of the Non-Aligned Movement, the UN General Assembly has declared 1990–99 the decade of international law. The main purpose of the declaration is to promote respect for the principles of international law and for the International Court of Justice.

In another positive development, the UN has requested the International Law Commission to explore the possibility of establishing an International Criminal Court to try person accused of engaging in "drug trafficking across national frontiers." The proposal, initiated by fifteen Caribbean nations, resembles House Concurrent Resolution 333, introduced by Congressmen Jim Leach and Bob Kastenmeier in 1988. This resolution urges the president of the United States to convene a multilateral conference to create an International Criminal Court, with jurisdiction over internationally recognized crimes of terrorism, genocide, and torture. In October 1990, Congress, primarily through the efforts of Senator Arlen Specter, adopted the resolution in modified form, requiring the president to explore the need for such a court and report back to Congress by October 1, 1991.

At the spring 1988 UN Special Session on Disarmament the Six Nation Initiative for an International Verification System was proposed by India, Sweden, Mexico, Argentina, Greece, and Tanzania. If approved, it would establish a UN organization to verify arms control agreements. As a multilateral agency it could act as a neutral party to investigate charges of cheating on agreements. It would get the United Nations involved in verifying steps towards disarmament and would be an important step in establishing a global security system.

In 1983, Representative George E. Brown, Jr., introduced a Common Security Resolution that advocates not only a comprehensive treaty for staged disarmament, but also stronger international peacekeeping institutions. This resolution had more than fifty sponsors in the House of Representatives. Senator Claiborne Pell introduced a companion resolution in 1984.

One positive development that may lead to many more is the passing of legislation creating a bipartisan U.S. Commission on Improving the Effectiveness of the United Nations. The commission may examine specific reform proposals, including proposals to redistribute power in the United Nations according to population and gross national product and to create permanent peacekeeping forces and an International Arms Control Verification Agency.

A March 1989 public opinion poll shows that most U.S. citizens support a stronger United Nations. Specifically, four out of five citizens surveyed believe that their government should adhere to adverse decisions of the World Court, rather than ignore such decisions, and that the United States should pay its full dues to the UN on a regular basis. Two out of three support giving the UN power to deal with global environmental problems, and three out of four support giving it the power to control the spread and manufacture of both chemical and nuclear weapons.[20]

Those who advocate outlawing war can cite many recent successes. The end of the cold war and the resulting ability to have the United Nations act in concert against aggression should provide hope to advocates of a stronger UN. Within the next five years we could succeed in establishing an International Criminal Court for international terrorists and global drug traffickers. We could establish a UN Environmental Agency that has the authority to enforce global environmental regulations, an International Verification System to verify compliance with arms reduction agreements, and a UN Peacekeeping Reserve.

The main organization supporting these activities to strengthen international institutions is the World Federalist Association, which has only four full-time and six part-time staff members and a membership of 8,000. Few people know about these positive steps and even fewer are supporting them.

6

■■■

Objections to the Proposal to Outlaw War

■■■

Many objections have been raised to the proposal to outlaw war. Among them: people don't want to be members of a minority in a larger political unit; people think that national defense is adequate for security and don't see a need to abolish war; enforced international law would require a world police force and we could have a global tyranny; under a world government we would no longer be Americans; we could never reach agreement anyway; the entire idea is naive.

Wouldn't We Be a Minority?

The biggest obstacles are the ones that rational people don't express, but that unfortunately many people feel. People fear being part of a larger political unit dominated by people of a different race or ideology. In a world government with "one person, one vote," Indians and Chinese would outnumber Japanese, Russians, Europeans, and North Americans. If the principle were "one country, one vote," the small Latin American, Asian, and African nations might have a majority.

But world federalism does not mean having everyone part of one world state but rather having a means to settle disputes between nations. It is true that the settling of international disputes can affect national life, and it is also true that accepting the principle of international authority in a few prescribed areas might prove to be a first step toward a world government.

The United States might find itself part of a larger political unit, most of whose members would not be of European background. Nor would most be Chinese, or Middle Eastern, or from any one background—a world federation would be a federation of minorities. To be effective the administrators of the world authority would have to attempt to be fair in their judgments and to respect the rights of all. Under an unjust authority, the federation would come apart long before evolving into a world government.

One goal of those who want to reform the United Nations is to find a voting formula that will fairly weigh three main factors. The first is population. Democracy demands some system whereby people elect representatives having equal numbers of constituents. The second factor is nations. The reality of nation states dictates that each nation should have representatives, regardless of its size. The third factor is wealth. If the richest nations contribute more than others, they want power proportional to their contributions.

One proposal for taking into account the facts of population, nations, and wealth calls for having three chambers in the United Nations. The first chamber would have each member representing the same number of people; the second chamber would have one representative from each nation; and the third chamber would have representatives proportional to financial contribution.

Federalists have considered various proposals for weighting the power of each chamber. For instance, a bill might pass only when two-thirds of each chamber support it, or only one chamber of elected representatives could be established, with their votes tallied according to nationality, population, and financial contribution to the United Nations.

What's Wrong with National Defense?

The purpose of national governments, according to Locke, Hobbes, and many others, is to protect citizens, yet modern military strategy is based on exposing citizens to danger. The balance of terror, Mutual Assured Destruction (MAD), is a gigantic system of hostages in which actually exchanging hostages is not necessary because Americans and Russians are within each other's grasp. Both governments tacitly agree, by pursuing a MAD policy, to expose their populations to their adversaries. It is paradoxical that nation states that base their justification on the need to protect their citizens expose their citizens to the possibility of annihilation.

If we forget about nationality for a moment and think in terms of people and governments, one could say that the governments of both the United States and the Soviet Union are endangering the citizens of both countries. On one side are people who want to be left alone to lead their lives, and on the other side are governments building armaments that make people less secure. The people on both sides would be better off without governments "protecting" them.

The notion that nation states can protect citizens in the nuclear age creates more paradoxes. No one believes that it is possible to ward off a nuclear attack against one's country, so it simply does not make sense to speak of national defense in the nuclear age. The best that military planners hope for is deterrence—if they have enough weapons to destroy the other side, the other side may be deterred from attacking.

The policy of deterrence has guided military policy for forty years—since the start of the atomic age. President Ronald Reagan called it into question with his proposal for a Strategic Defense Initiative (SDI), better known as Star Wars, an attempt to defend the United States with devices that would intercept any incoming missiles. The problem with SDI is that there is no reason to think that it would work or that we could afford the billions—perhaps trillions—of dollars it would require. Instead, SDI would start a new arms race and make the Soviet Union fear a first strike because it would appear that the United States was preparing to survive a nuclear war. This fear, compounded by development of the Stealth bomber that flies below radar, would force decision making to become quicker and more dependent upon computers. Worse still, SDI assumes that the problem of security is technical, when in fact it is social and political.

Nations can only provide security for their citizens by accepting an international authority to settle their disputes with other nations. If nations are to perform their most basic function, then they should pursue policies that enhance the security of their citizens. Since security cannot be provided at the national level, governments should pursue security by transcending nationality. The only way that governments can perform their function of providing security is by transcending themselves and working to strengthen an international authority.

The idea that one nation has the right to decide the just settlement of its disputes with other nations is ludicrous. As a party to the conflict it cannot be objective. Furthermore, any conflict in the world can potentially affect every other nation, so the claim of one nation to settle conflicts without involving the international community cannot be accepted by other nations. In the interest of peace, every nation must give up its claim to be judge, jury, and executioner in international conflicts.

Doesn't World Law Require a World Police Force?

A common response to the proposal to outlaw war is that it is a fine but unworkable goal. People who say this believe that, before there can be enforceable international law, all the nations would have to give their armaments to an international authority, which would then be the only force with weapons. They don't see any possibility of this happening, so they don't see how war could be outlawed. I also don't see nations disarming to create a supranational military force, but I believe that outlawing war does not require such an action.

Critics of the proposal to outlaw war believe that enforceable world law cannot work because, like most people, they think that the party making laws must have a monopoly on military power to enforce those laws. This view, articulated by the nineteenth-century jurist John Austin, is known as the Command Theory of Law.

Austin believed that "to affirm of laws universally 'that they flow from *superiors*'; or to affirm of laws universally 'that *inferiors* are bound to obey them,' is the merest tautology and trifling" because "the term *superiority* signifies *might*: the power of affecting others with evil or pain, and of forcing them through fear of that evil, to fashion their conduct to one's wishes."[21] The theory assumes that law is imposed on the powerless by the powerful, a view people accept when they assume that the enforcement of international law would require a supreme international army.

The Command Theory of Law leads to some absurdities, which is, of course, a good reason to reject it. For example, a sovereign who has a monopoly on power can punish those who obey the law, and let those who break the law go unpunished, and no one can stop the sovereign. I would not say that such a society is ruled by law. Austin's theory thus contradicts our common sense notions of what it means to live in a society that is ruled by law.

For a society to be ruled by law at least two conditions must hold. Those who break the law must be punished, and those who obey the law must be left alone. While the power to mete out punishment is given to sovereigns, the requirement that law abiding citizens be left alone is a limitation on the power of sovereigns. Since enforcement of law cannot be understood to involve people's limiting their own power, the enforcement of law involves an interaction of forces.

The force that makes law enforceable need not be military. As Roger Fischer, a professor of law at Harvard University, observes, "When a judgment is entered against the United States in the Court of Claims, no superior sovereign compels Congress to vote the appropriation. Legal limitations upon a government, whether they be those of constitutional law or international law, succeed or fail for reasons other than the existence of superior military force. By and large law with respect to governments works because it affects political consequences, not military ones."[22]

International law can come about by an interaction of forces. It does not require the existence of one international group with a monopoly of power. As I have argued, if one group had a monopoly of power there would be no enforcement of law, which depends on a plurality of forces. Law is like a boundary between parties, and enforcement depends on the ability of parties to coerce respect for the boundary, a power that is usually political and not military.

One implication of this view is that the ability to enforce laws is not a property of the sovereign.[23] We can imagine one group passing laws and another group enforcing those laws. There could be a world government without a world military force. We might, for example, envision a group like the United Nations passing laws that were enforced by citizens living in the member states, rather than by governments or by a supranational government. Taxes would be enforced by people in each nation who insist that their national leaders pay taxes or be ousted. Thus people in the member states would act to support international law by taking actions against their government if their nation disobeyed that law.

The ability of ordinary citizens to help enforce international law is demonstrated in the battle against apartheid. The United Nations has condemned apartheid and citizens are seeing to it that the UN-imposed sanctions against South Africa are enforced, by refusing to do business with South Africa or by insuring that their cities, pension funds, and businesses refuse to do business with South Africa.

The first step towards international law is to have an international organization pass laws whose enforcement requires that leaders either comply or are punished. Enforcement of an order to remove troops from the territory of another nation occurs if enough people are willing to force their nation to comply. Enforcement might also occur if people in other nations impose a trade boycott. There are as many ways to enforce international law as there are sanctions that can be applied, and it does not matter who is applying the sanctions.

An international authority might be established either by national governments or by individuals. National leaders cannot protect citizens, so they should seek international authority to provide security, and if they do not, individuals should bypass them. Individuals have a right to pledge their allegiance to an international authority that can provide security. However international authority is established, its enforcement depends upon individual citizens who either pressure national leaders or bypass them.

Couldn't We Have a Global Tyranny?

Some people who object to the idea of world peace through world law do so because they envision a world authority doing the same things a nation does, only on a larger scale. People are suspicious of governments for good reason. Governments wage wars and sometimes oppress their own people. How do we know that having a world authority won't just mean more militarism and more oppression?

One reason to speak of world federalism instead of world government is to separate desirable from less desirable visions of world order. Favoring world federalism means favoring a particular form of world government. The world federalist vision is for a demilitarized and decentralized world.

A world federation on the community model would be closer to the anarchist dream of a world without coercion than to any tyranny that has existed, if by "anarchy" we mean not the contention of political forces to fill a power vacuum, but the maintenance of a power vacuum. It is rule without a ruler, for no one ruler controls all areas and power is dispersed over separate non-government organizations.

If a federation of the world's nations existed and war were outlawed, the world authority would require fewer weapons than any state now has, and even fewer as nations disarm. States have weapons to protect themselves from invasion by other states. Once an authority is accepted for the settling of disputes, nations would no longer need to spend more on weapons than one of the fifty American states spends on its militia. The level of government with the most armaments holds sovereignty and is in conflict with other sovereign forces. Local and state governments do not have armaments because they cannot go to war with each other. National governments have armaments because they are allowed to declare war. If nation states could no longer go to war, but, instead, had to submit their disputes to an international legal system, then the nation states would no longer need armaments. The international authority would need police powers to enforce law, but would not need the level of armaments that nation states now have because there would be no other international authority to fight.

How can someone who wants to outlaw war reply to a person who believes that military force is needed to protect liberty? One reply is that the option of force is taken away from all parties, not just the United States. When the rule of law replaces force, one uses fact and argument to win one's way, instead of military might.

The issue is whether it is better to replace force and fraud, the methods of war, with fact and reason, the methods of law. I believe that facts and reason favor liberty, and that when people can make decisions according to these methods, people choose in favor of liberty. Force and fraud can be used as well, if not better, by the enemies of liberty.

Would We No Longer Be Americans?

The only sovereignty that nations have to give up to achieve peace is sovereignty in international affairs. Nations such as the United States and the Soviet Union would have to give up their claim to the right to determine the future of other countries such as Vietnam and El Salvador, Poland and Afghanistan. Nations would still maintain the right to do as they liked within their own territory, and thus they would keep their national sovereignty. But they would have to give up their prerogative to act as international sovereigns.

Talk of world government only confuses the essential issues. Peace does not require a world government that replaces national governments. Nations can continue as they are now in every respect but one: disputes between them would have to be brought before an international authority.

If the world survives into the twenty-first century and people look back on human history, they will see a development from tribal units to clans to communities, to nations and, finally, to an international community. They will be puzzled at why we hesitated so long—almost too long—at the nation-state level. When they view our history and learn that we did not even have nation states until a few hundred years ago, and read of all the sorrow that nations and their wars have caused humanity they will be puzzled at our obstinacy. The growth beyond the nation-state level will seem to them a natural step, as natural as were the steps from family to clan, and from clan to community. All these previous steps will appear as preparation for the forming of a global community.

The solution to the problem of war is for nations to give up part of their sovereignty when they have disputes with other nations and accept the judgments of an international legal system. Why don't nations do this? There is a price to the achievement of peace. That price is the giving up of some foolish ideas—that nations can provide protection for their citizens in the nuclear age, that nations can settle conflicts by themselves without an international authority, that nations have sovereignty in international affairs. When you consider that all these ideas are false anyway, the price of peace is not very great.

We Could Never Reach Agreement Anyway

Anyone who thinks that the United States and the Soviet Union cannot come to an agreement on general and complete disarmament doesn't know about the McCloy-Zorin Agreement. In 1961 Premier Nikita Krushchev and President John F. Kennedy gave negotiators the task of developing a framework for general and complete disarmament. John J. McCloy and Arthur H. Dean for the United States, and Valerian Zorin for the Soviet Union, negotiated for five months and produced a Joint Statement on Agreement of Principles for Disarmament Negotiations, which was submitted to the UN General Assembly on September 20, 1961.

Difficulties arose, of course, in the negotiations. The main problem was allowing inspection within the borders of both countries. The Soviet Union was willing to allow inspection to verify the destruction of specific weapons and production facilities but was not willing to open the entire country up to inspection, the main obstacle in 1962. In retrospect, we know why. If the Soviets had allowed inspection, the Americans would have discovered that they enjoyed better than a ten-to-one advantage in nuclear weapons. Today, with the differences in weapons much less, the Soviet Union is more open to inspection.

A Common Security resolution based on the McCloy-Zorin Agreement has been sponsored by Representative George E. Brown, a Democrat from California. The World Federalist Association, and some other groups that favor world peace through world law, supports this resolution and other attempts to insure that the agreement is not forgotten. A summary of the agreement as it appears in Mr. Brown's resolution follows.

(1) The international agreement should specify the sequence for disarming all nations, by stages, and the time limits for each stage.

(2) The international agreement, with the understanding of all parties that the nature and extent of control will depend on the verification required for each stage, should provide such strict and effective international control at all stages that all parties could be assured that all other parties are complying with the agreement.

(3) An international security and disarmament authority should be established with its own voting procedures within the framework of the United Nations, to implement control over the inspection of disarmament.

(4) The international security and disarmament authority should have its own inspectors who should have unrestricted access without veto to all necessary places for verification at each stage of the disarmament process and its own international peacekeeping surveillance system, using the best available satellite surveillance technology.

(5) The disarmament process should proceed in such a manner that at no point could any nation or group of nations gain military advantage, and equal security is insured for all.

(6) There should be agreement among all parties before each subsequent stage in the disarmament process is begun that the preceding stage has been implemented and verified in a satisfactory manner and that any additional verification arrangements required for the next stage are ready.

(7) Progress in disarmament should be accompanied by measures to create new institutions, and to strengthen existing ones, for maintaining the peace and resolving all international disputes by peaceful means.

(8) The nations participating in the negotiations for an international agreement should strive to achieve and implement the widest possible agreement at the earliest possible date and should continue their efforts without interruption until agreement upon the total program has been achieved.

(9) Nuclear-free zones and existing treaties and agreements should be preserved and expanded as part of the negotiating process and efforts on other arms control and disarmament measures should continue in a manner designed to facilitate negotiations on the international agreement.[24]

Isn't the Notion of Outlawing War Naive?

There is nothing naive in arguing for world federalism. Those who think that we can continue to have an arms race and wars without ending up with a nuclear exchange are naive. It is naive to think that nations will give up the use of military force when there is no way to insure that conflicts will be settled without force. World federalists do not hold any of these naive assumptions.

World federalists do hope that people can recognize that today we are facing the threat of annihilation. Just as most states throughout history were formed through force, a federation of the world's nations will be formed because of the tremendous force that will be unleashed against humanity if we do not abolish war.

Law is the alternative to war. Just as the rule of law replaces war within a country, it can replace war in the international arena. When all nations are part of an international legal system, any nation that believes it is being wronged can redress that wrong through a court system with full assurance that every nation is bound by the ruling of the international tribunal.

Apart from the removal of the danger of war and the expense of armaments, the average person's life would not change very much. Under an international authority, those who travel would find it much easier to do so, and there would be more world trade. People would still elect their mayors and city councils, governors and state legislatures, the president of their nation and their representatives to Congress. Perhaps people would also be able to elect a world president.

Part III

Providing Security

John Trever, *Albuquerque Journal*

■ The release of atomic energy has created a
world in which the old ways of thinking,
that include old diplomatic conventions and
balance-of-power politics, have become utterly
meaningless. Mankind must give up war in the
atomic era. What is at stake is the life or death
of humanity.

— Albert Einstein

7

∎∎∎

Military Advantage
in the Nuclear Age

∎∎∎

The Persian Gulf War demonstrated that the United States is currently the world's predominant military power. A new generation of weapons capable of pin-point accuracy was displayed on television. The Allied Forces suffered fewer than two hundred casualties in destroying the world's fourth largest army. The United States hasn't experienced such overwhelming military superiority since dropping the atomic bomb. Can maintaining military superiority provide security or other benefits? To answer this question we must learn from the past, from the beginning of the nuclear age.

At the onset of the nuclear age leaders assumed that having more powerful weapons meant having more political power. The United States dropped atomic bombs on Japan to show the Soviet Union its military superiority and used that superiority to make the Soviets back down in the Cuban missile crisis. But the advantages won by military superiority were not as great as anticipated. Nuclear weapons proved different from previous weapons. In the age of overkill, a nation cannot destroy other nations without being destroyed. The United States recognized this by signing the Anti-Ballistic Missile Treaty and accepting the view that all sides are equally vulnerable. The war game is one that no one can win.

Dropping the Bomb on Japan

Every year on the anniversary of the dropping of the atomic bomb people debate the wisdom of President Harry Truman's decision.

It is amazing that anyone still claims that it was necessary to drop the bomb in order to end the war or save American lives. An invasion of Japan was not scheduled until spring 1946, with a preliminary invasion of the island of Kyushu scheduled for November. The Soviet Union's entering the war against Japan in August was expected to bring about Japan's surrender. On July 17, when Stalin confirmed that the Soviet Union would declare war against Japan, President Truman wrote in his diary, "Fini Japs when that comes about."[1] Truman knew, both by intercepting the cable, and because Stalin gave the message to him, that the emperor of Japan was sending his personal envoy to Moscow "to convey to the Soviet Government that it was exclusively the desire of His Majesty to avoid more bloodshed."[2]

Those who were involved and understood the military situation were unanimous in their judgment that the bomb was not necessary. General Dwight Eisenhower stated that "it wasn't necessary to hit them with that awful thing." The chief of staff, Admiral William D. Leahy, stated, "It is my opinion that the use of this barbarous weapon at Hiroshima was of no material assistance in our war against Japan. The Japanese were already defeated and ready to surrender because of the effective sea blockade and the successful bombing with conventional weapons."[3]

To understand the dropping of atomic bombs on Japan we must understand what was happening in Central Europe. Winston Churchill had accepted Soviet predominance in Hungary, Bulgaria, and Rumania in return for British predominance in Greece and joint responsibility in Yugoslavia, at least until formal peace treaties with new governments could be signed. In October 1944, President Franklin Roosevelt had told Churchill and the USSR's Joseph Stalin, "I am most pleased that you are reaching a meeting of your two minds," indicating that he consented to the de facto spheres of influence.[4] President Truman wanted to reverse Roosevelt's policy and to insure free elections in the Balkan nations.

Truman, Churchill, and Stalin agreed to have a meeting at Potsdam, Germany, to discuss postwar arrangements in Europe and to enlist Soviet aid in the war against Japan. Truman expected to have a showdown with Stalin over arrangements in Europe, and he didn't want this showdown until he had something he thought would insure his victory. Meanwhile, Stalin kept demanding that the United States recognize the new governments in the Balkans.[5]

On June 19, 1946, Truman replied, "I am giving this matter further study. . . . I therefore propose that we discuss it at our forthcoming meeting." Stalin insisted again, right before Potsdam, "there is no justification for further delay in resuming diplomatic relations with Rumania and Bulgaria."[6] Truman postponed the Potsdam meeting to give the physicists more time. He expected the atomic bomb to help him in his confrontation with Stalin.

The first successful atomic test occurred on the first morning of the Potsdam Conference, July 16. Secretary of War Henry Stimson gave President Truman a report on the bomb and recorded in his diary, "He said it gave him an entirely new feeling of confidence and he thanked me for having come to the Conference and being present to help him in this way." A day later Stimson read the same report to Churchill, who responded, "Now I know what happened to Truman yesterday. I couldn't understand it. When he got to the meeting after having read this report he was a changed man. He told the Russians just where they got on and off and generally bossed the whole meeting."[7]

In addition to wanting to force the Soviet Union to withdraw its troops in Eastern Europe, Truman also wanted to keep the Soviets from gaining control of Manchuria. Secretary of State James Byrnes had told Truman months before the bombing of Hiroshima that "the bomb might well put us in a position to dictate our own terms at the end of the war." After dropping the bomb, Truman wrote, "This is the greatest thing in history!" He believed that "Our dropping of the atomic bomb on Japan had forced Russia to reconsider her position in the Far East."[8]

The United States may have developed the atomic bomb as a defensive effort, but it was not dropped for defense purposes and the United States does not continue building weapons purely for defense purposes. The fact is that Japan was in no condition to continue the fighting and was approaching the United States to discuss terms for surrender. Having atomic weapons was and continues to be seen as a method for advancing U.S. national interests.

The Arms Race before the Cuban Missile Crisis

From 1945 to 1949, the United States was the only nation to have atomic weapons. The country's failure to attack the Soviet Union when it had a monopoly on nuclear weapons is not necessarily evidence of good intentions, however. At the time, the United States did not have enough weapons to do more than hurt the Russians, and the Soviet Union could have retaliated with conventional forces in Europe.

After U.S. bombs failed to stop the Soviet Union in Eastern Europe, American military planners might have concluded that atomic weapons do not allow the advantages that leaders at first expected. Instead they concluded that they needed more bombs, and for the first ten years of the atomic era the United States held an arms race with itself.

Despite being the only nation with the bomb, and despite the absence of any reason to believe that other nations would get the bomb soon, the United States built several hundred atomic bombs between 1945 and 1949—before the Soviet Union exploded its first atom bomb. During the late forties, the United States also built bases for B-29 bombers in Greenland, Iceland, Okinawa, Alaska, and Japan, so that the Soviet Union could be attacked using nuclear weapons.

In 1948, still before the Soviet Union had the atomic bomb, the United States introduced the first intercontinental bombers. The Soviet Union did not have an intercontinental bomber until 1954. After the Soviet Union tested its first atomic bomb in 1949, the United States tested the first hydrogen bomb in 1952. The Soviet Union tested a hydrogen bomb in 1955.

After 1957 the arms race became a two-way affair, but the Soviet Union did not try to match the United States in number of weapons until after the Cuban missile crisis. In 1957 the Soviet Union introduced its first new weapon in the arms race—the Intercontinental Ballistic Missile (ICBM), a step that was matched by the United States in 1958. Two months after firing the first ICBM, the Soviet Union launched the first satellite, Sputnik. The United States launched its first satellite in 1958.

Even though the United States had a decisive military advantage over the Soviet Union at the beginning of the arms race, national leaders spoke of weapons gaps in order to get more weapons. In 1950, President Truman's National Security Council produced National Security Council Paper No. 68, which called for "an immediate and large scale building of our military and general strength and that of our allies with the intention of righting the balance of power." At that time the Soviet Union had exploded one atomic bomb and with no long-range bombers had no way to drop bombs on the United States. The United States had several hundred atomic bombs and bomber bases circling the Soviet Union.

In 1954 at its May Day celebration the Soviet Union unveiled its first intercontinental bomber, the Bison. For the first time the United States was vulnerable to Soviet weapons, just as the Soviet Union had been vulnerable for many years. A special presidential commission was formed to deal with the "bomber gap" and the intercontinental ballistic missile program was given the highest priority. At the time there was a gap, only it went the other way. The United States had five bombers for every one the Soviets had. Talk of a bomber gap quickly switched to talk of a "missile gap" after the Soviet Union tested an intercontinental ballistic missile in August 1957.

In 1960, John Kennedy campaigned on the claim that there was a missile gap. During the campaign he claimed that the Soviet Union had between three hundred and a thousand intercontinental ballistic missiles. Actually the Soviet Union had between fifty and one hundred. The United States, with more than one hundred intercontinental ballistic missiles at home and missile bases circling the Soviet Union, was capable of delivering five thousand nuclear weapons to the Soviets' four hundred. The talk of a gap was nonsense. Former president Richard Nixon later stated, "At the time of the Cuban missile crisis in 1962, the United States still had an overwhelming nuclear superiority, in the range of 15 to 1 or even more."[9]

The Cuban Missile Crisis

In April 1961, the U.S. Central Intelligence Agency under the direction of President Kennedy supported an invasion of Cuba at the Bay of Pigs. The invasion failed, but Fidel Castro and his Soviet allies had every reason to fear another invasion. At Cuba's request, the Soviet Union agreed to place missiles in Cuba.

On October 14, U.S. U-2 reconnaissance planes found evidence that the Soviet Union was deploying missiles in Cuba capable of hitting most American cities. On October 23, 1962, President Kennedy appeared on television and announced that, to "quarantine" Cuba, American ships were going to intercept Soviet ships in international waters, which is of course an act of war. President Kennedy's proclamation stated, "I, John F. Kennedy . . . do hereby proclaim that the forces under my command are ordered, beginning . . . October 24, 1962 . . . to interdict . . . the delivery of offensive weapons and associated material to Cuba." Chairman Khrushchev of the Soviet Union responded, "The actions of the USA with regard to Cuba are outright banditry" and he warned that if any efforts were made to interfere with Soviet ships "we would then be forced to take the measures we deem necessary and adequate in order to protect our rights."[10]

An exchange of communications followed the imposing of the blockade on Cuba. On October 26 Chairman Khrushchev proposed a trade that would have the Soviet Union "remove the weapons from Cuba which you regard as offensive weapons . . . and . . . the United States . . . evacuate its analogous weapons from Turkey." Under the proposed trade, the Soviet Government would "give a solemn pledge to respect the integrity of the frontiers and the sovereignty of Turkey . . . and the U.S. Government will make the same statement in the Security Council with regard to Cuba."[11]

Giving up the missiles in Turkey in a quid pro quo for the missiles in Cuba would not have affected the strategic balance of forces. They were obsolete Jupiter missiles that were scheduled for removal anyway and indeed were removed soon afterward separate from any agreement. Even the Cuban missiles were not important to any strategic balance. During the October 16 meeting President Kennedy had questioned, "What difference does it make; they have enough missiles [within their borders] to blow us up anyway."[12] He nevertheless rejected the advice of his brother, Attorney General Robert Kennedy, and Secretary of State Dean Rusk to accept a trade.

On October 27 the Soviet Union repeated its offer, but the United States continued the blockade of Cuba. Tensions were then rising because the Soviet Union used a missile to shoot down a U-2 spy plane over Cuba. At one point the president's advisors voted to strike at the missile base but then decided to try other steps first. The FBI reported that preparations had been made at the Soviet embassy to shred documents and Defense Secretary Robert S. McNamara reported that Russians at the missile base in Cuba were working day and night getting the missiles ready.[13]

Members of Kennedy's advisory committee left their meeting on October 27 thinking that they were starting a third world war. According to Robert Kennedy, "The president was not optimistic, nor was I. . . . The expectation was a military confrontation by Tuesday [October 30]." John Kennedy realized that his actions could end life on earth. According to his brother, "The thought that disturbed him the most, and that made the prospect of war much more fearful than it would otherwise have been, was the specter of the death of the children of this country and the world."[14]

The Soviet ships turned back at the last minute and war was avoided. At a 1989 gathering, Cuban missile crisis participants revealed that those who were close to the decisions had thought war might occur.[15] On October 27, Khrushchev's personal assistant and a member of the Central Committee had moved their families out of Moscow because they expected a nuclear attack. McNamara had left the President's office thinking that he might never live to see another Saturday night. Cuban officials at the time estimated that a U.S. strike on the missiles would have cost 100,000 lives, and the Soviets say they would have responded by attacking the U.S. Jupiter missiles in Turkey.

Assessments of Kennedy's action differ. According to Graham Allison, former dean of the Kennedy School of Government at Harvard, Kennedy's action was "one of the finest examples of diplomatic prudence and perhaps the finest hour of John F. Kennedy's presidency." The view that I accept comes from Noam Chomsky, a linguist at MIT, who has referred to Kennedy's action as "the lowest point in human history."[16]

President Kennedy's actions during the Cuban missile crisis were certainly popular. At the time, I worked for a peace candidate, Stuart Hughes, a Harvard professor who ran for the U.S. Senate against John Kennedy's brother Ted. When Hughes criticized President Kennedy's actions and suggested that Khrushchev be offered a face-saving trade, public opinion polls showed him losing half his supporters.

The Arms Race after the Cuban Missile Crisis

The Soviet Union changed its policy on armaments after losing face in the Cuban missile crisis. Although before the crisis the Soviets had showed no interest in trying to match the United States, at a meeting to discuss the removal of missiles, Soviet Foreign Minister Vasily Kuznetsov told an American negotiator, "You Americans will never be able to do this to us again."[17]

The Soviet Union learned from the crisis that they needed more weapons so that the United States would not push them around. They assumed, as did the Americans, that military superiority meant political power and thus engaged in a huge arms build-up. Now the two superpowers are roughly equal in weapons.

Military Superiority and Nuclear Weapons

Building more advanced weapons does not provide permanent advantages. The competition quickly catches up. The United States introduced the atomic bomb and the hydrogen bomb, and the Soviet Union caught up. The Soviet Union introduced intercontinental ballistic missiles and anti-ballistic missiles, and the United States caught up. Instead of gaining an advantage, all that has been accomplished is a world filled with bombs that can destroy us all.

When two nations can each destroy the other, it does not make sense to speak of one being militarily superior to the other. The old ways of thinking simply do not work; the old concepts no longer apply.

If war is defined as an unlimited conflict that has winners and losers, then in the modern world war is impossible. One of the greatest military theorists of all time, the Prussian general Karl von Clausewitz wrote, "War is an act of force, and there is no limit to the application of that force. Each of the adversaries forces the hand of the other, and a reciprocal action results which theoretically can have no limit."[18]

The Vietnam War can be cited as an example in which a nuclear nation decided to lose a war rather than use its nuclear weapons. Our national survival was not threatened by Vietnam. If a nuclear nation's existence were threatened and it had a choice of losing a war or using its atomic arsenal, it would probably use its arsenal. Once two nuclear powers started using atomic weapons they would believe their existence threatened and an escalation could occur. That possibility makes modern warfare impossible between nuclear powers.

If people used all their energy in a confrontation today, the energy of the atom would destroy us all. As Jonathan Schell, staff writer for the *New Yorker* and author of *The Fate of the Earth*, observes, "Traditional military doctrine began . . . with the premise that the amounts of force available to the belligerents were small enough to permit one side or the other to exhaust itself before both sides were annihilated. Nuclear doctrine, on the other hand, begins with the premise that the amounts of force are so great that both sides, and perhaps all mankind, will be annihilated before either side exhausts its forces."[19]

If war is defined as an unlimited conflict that has winners and losers, then in the modern world war is impossible. It is not impossible because the suffering of survivors would be intolerable—it is impossible because there would be no survivors. An exchange of all force that is available would mean the death of all, which is more correctly called omnicide rather than war.

More and more people are coming to realize that military superiority offers no advantage when each side can destroy the other. That each side is vulnerable to the other and that one side can only be secure if the other is secure was recognized in the Anti-Ballistic Missile Treaty, which states, "Each party undertakes not to deploy ABM systems for the defense of the territory of its country and not to provide a base for such defense."[20]

We have recognized that once nations have atomic weapons we cannot dominate them by having superior weapons. Yet nuclear nations continue to dominate nonnuclear nations. The United States would never have acted as it did in Vietnam, Libya, Nicaragua, Grenada, Panama, and Iraq if those nations had had nuclear weapons. The Soviet Union and other Warsaw Pact nations would never have invaded Czechoslovakia and Hungary if those nations had had the bomb. That is, of course, one reason why nations are rushing to get the bomb.

The advantages that nuclear nations enjoy will end as more nations have the atomic bomb. Nations that definitely have the bomb are the United States, the Soviet Union, France, Britain, China, India, and Israel. Two nations that are thought to have the bomb are South Africa and Taiwan. By 1995 another forty-five nations will join the list, and by 2010 more than one hundred nations could have atomic weapons. Membership in the atomic club will no longer bestow privileges, and, after some rowdy newcomers like Libya and Iraq join the club, the old members will want to dissolve it. A new impetus toward arms control will emerge from the realization that most nations will have atomic weapons.

What will things be like when a nation like Libya has nuclear weapons? Colonel Muammar Kaddafi has given us some indication. Referring to the U.S. bombing of Tripoli and Benghazi in 1986, Libya's news agency reported that Kaddafi said, "If we had a deterrent force of missiles able to reach New York we would have directed them at that very moment. We therefore must have this force so that the Americans and others would not think to attack us once again."[21]

Dismissing his words would be easy if Kaddafi were thinking like a madman. What is really frightening is that Kaddafi makes the same assumptions that we make. He is assuming that rights are conferred on nations according to their military might. The United States bombed Kaddafi's home to retaliate for a bombing that killed American soldiers in a Berlin disco. The Reagan administration thought that Libya was responsible. Our bombs killed Kaddafi's fifteen-month-old daughter and wounded two of his sons.[22] What gave the United States the right to bomb Libya? Israel claims to have evidence that links Syria to an attempted bombing of an El Al airliner in London, and Great Britain and West Germany suspect Syria in that incident and also in a Berlin bombing.[23] Why don't we bomb Syria? Is it because Syria has a defense pact with the Soviet Union and Libya has no nuclear umbrella? When we act as if our having the atomic bomb gives us the right to act as we want towards nonnuclear nations, it is no wonder that they want the bomb.

Would we have bombed Libya if it had had atomic weapons? Would we have bombed Hanoi if North Vietnam could have used atomic weapons on New York? Would we have invaded Grenada or Panama if those nations had atomic weapons? By taking actions we would not take if other nations had atomic arsenals we give those nations an incentive to develop atomic weapons.

Our victory in the Persian Gulf War would not have been possible if the Iraqis possessed long-range nuclear missiles. Once the new technology that allowed us to destroy Iraq's air defenses spreads, our own air defenses will be obsolete. It is only a matter of time before more nations get nuclear weapons and develop their own "smart bombs," and then we will be less secure.

When every nation has atomic weapons, the advantages of having them disappear. The smallest nations will be able to endanger the largest. It will no longer be possible to use force in international affairs. If we are to survive, a new method of interactions will have to replace the old. The facts will dictate the rule, "One should treat every nation as though it had the power to destroy you." This will lead us to following the golden rule, "One should behave towards others as he would want them to behave towards him."[24] As is often the case, people will end up doing the right thing only after everything else has failed.

8

...

Deterrence and the Strategic Defense Initiative

...

All roads lead to the unknown. Advocates of the Strategic Defense Initiative (SDI) and others have pointed out the faults of the current deterrence policy. The SDI was originally presented as a complete shield that would protect the United States from nuclear missiles. Now, no one claims it is a complete defense system. If it is not complete, all it does is enhance deterrence, assuming the other side does not just build more missiles. For the SDI to enhance defense, both sides must agree to embark on a switch from counterpopulation to counterforce weapons in a way that allays fear of a first strike. I believe that such steps, unlike anything attempted before, would be more difficult and less likely to occur than the abolition of war.

Disgust with Deterrence

Given the goal of preventing the use of nuclear weapons, the issue becomes how best to do it. The strategy adopted by both the United States and the Soviet Union is called deterrence, and the theory behind it is that if all the major powers have nuclear weapons, each will be deterred from using its weapons for fear of retaliation. To make the threat of retaliation real, nations must both have weapons and be willing to use them.

The deterrence strategy is paradoxical in that it requires

preparing for a holocaust that no one wants and building nuclear weapons that no one will ever use. Following the deterrence strategy, we try to attain security by threatening ourselves with extinction. We build weapons that we hope never to use, but which we must be committed to use.

That it requires us to have weapons that could destroy all life on the planet should provide us with ample reason to question the wisdom of deterrence. The mere fact that the planet is now holding weapons that could annihilate us makes us less secure. A nuclear holocaust could be set off by any of the world's leaders, or by a computer error.

Deterrence theory assumes that a nation once attacked would be willing to use its nuclear weapons. Suppose that a nation is attacked with nuclear weapons. Why should it strike back? The purpose of having nuclear weapons was to prevent other nations from attacking. But suppose they did attack? What purpose would striking back serve? After being attacked, one's own country would be a radioactive wasteland. Only a few leaders in underground shelters and special planes would survive. With their own nation destroyed, why would these few survivors want to destroy the rest of the planet?

The actual nuclear strategies of nations are confused, although proponents of deterrence will claim that the reason they have weapons is to deter attack from others. Nations use nuclear weapons to their advantage in their dealings with other nations, and they speak and act in ways that contradict their stated deterrence policies. The superpowers, for example, speak of being "first" in weapons when being a secondary power is all that is needed for deterrence. They spend money on civil defense, whereas deterrence assumes that both sides will be vulnerable. Now the superpowers are developing counterforce weapons aimed at each other's weapons, which would jeopardize retaliation.

A consistent deterrence policy would openly expose the populations of all major powers to annihilation. No nation would attempt to be first in weapons. No money would be spent on civil defense. Only weapons aimed at destroying industries and population centers would be developed. A nation interested only in deterrence would stop building weapons once enough were amassed to destroy the main population centers of any would-be attacker. Neither the United States nor the USSR follow a pure deterrence policy.

Americans should question whether weapons exist for security or for some other purpose. It is one thing to risk our lives so that we may deter an attack; it is another to risk our lives so that the United States may continue to use nuclear weapons to enhance its political power.

The people of our planet have reached an impasse on methods of providing security. We pay homage to deterrence, but we are really not satisfied with this approach, as evidenced by civil defense and attempts to develop counterforce weapons. Our weapons make us less secure.

The policy of Mutual Assured Destruction was accepted by accident, not by design. The choice of military strategy has always been dependent on the technology available. This was so during World War II when Britain and the United States debated the choice between using tactical or strategic bombing against Germany. Tactical bombing is used to support troops with localized bombing against military targets. Strategic bombing is used to undermine a nation's war effort and morale with widespread bombing against transportation centers, munitions factories, shipyards, and, if deemed useful, civilians. Because the bombsights on British aircraft were not accurate enough, at the height they had to fly for safety, to allow them to hit only military targets, the decision was to use strategic bombing, despite the traditional belief that noncombatants should be spared the ravages of war.[25] After the war this translated into a strategy of aiming bombs at cities. Now, with weapons that make possible a tactical defense system, and with enough bombs aimed at population centers to annihilate humanity, many people believe that we made a colossal mistake in pursuing the strategic course. The problem is whether we should try to switch at this point to a tactical defense system.

The Strategic Defense Initiative

President Reagan's Strategic Defense Initiative was presented as a system to protect us against strategic weapons—the weapons aimed at our cities. In his March 23, 1983, address to the nation he said,

> If the Soviet Union will join with us in our efforts to achieve major arms reduction, we will have succeeded in stabilizing the nuclear balance. Nevertheless, it will still be necessary to rely on the specter of retaliation, on mutual threat. And that's a sad commentary on the human condition. Wouldn't it be better to save lives than to avenge them? . . .

After careful consultation with my advisers . . . I believe there is a way. Let me share with you a vision of the future which offers hope. It is that we embark on a program to counter the awesome Soviet missile threat with measures that are defensive. . . .

What if free people could live secure in the knowledge that their security did not rest upon the threat of instant U.S. retaliation to deter a Soviet attack, that we could intercept and destroy ballistic missiles before they reached our own soil or that of our allies?[26]

That the main impetus for the current desire for the SDI is a moral one is clear from President Reagan's speech. It is apparent that the current policy of Mutual Assured Destruction could annihilate humanity or, at the very least, kill millions of innocent people. Some believe that it would be preferable to have weapons aimed at other weapons than at people.

Many criticisms of the arms race made by people in the peace movement are now almost universally accepted. Everyone agrees that it is insane to have bombs aimed at each other's cities, that it is unjust to hold the populations of both countries hostage. Those who plan our defense like to think that they have a moral calling. They would like to change the current strategic strategy to a tactical one, a change they believe would answer many of the criticisms leveled against planning for nuclear war and provide a just system of defense.

The SDI can be understood as an attempt to overcome some of the moral problems of deterrence doctrine, which had violated many of our notions of the just use of military force. Examining the fifteen-hundred-year-old just war tradition that began with Saint Augustine will show what is wrong with deterrence doctrine and how the SDI is morally superior.

The just war tradition judges methods of warfare according to whether they allow their user to discriminate between combatants and noncombatants, and whether they allow proportionate use of force so that more good than evil can be achieved. It was possible to apply the just war tradition to warfare up to the Age of Napoleon. War in the Middle Ages was limited to knights, who left noncombatants alone. Later, the use of guns allowed their users to discriminate between combatants and noncombatants. In the past one hundred years, since the time of Napoleon, warfare has taken a turn towards total war that engulfs civilians.

Many argue a return to the path of limited war to be both possible and desirable. Given a choice between the existing counterpopulation weapons and counterforce weapons with smaller pay-loads aimed more accurately, just war theory favors tactical weapons. Whether these weapons should be nuclear is an issue beyond the theory. Today's weapons are so accurate that the need for nuclear weapons disappears, except when bombing against hardened silos. Advocates of the SDI argue that by replacing strategic weapons with tactical ones—building down—we can reduce the destructive forces in the world.

Those who advocate the development of tactical weapons want to create options short of strategic nuclear war. Such options can be enhanced by building up conventional forces and switching to a tactical nuclear policy. Just war tradition cannot answer the question of whether a switch to tactical weapons would increase the chance of war by making a first strike possible, or whether the cost of a switch is prohibitive. The conclusion that a tactical defense strategy can be morally justified is irrelevant if a switch increases the risk of war or is prohibitively expensive, or if waging limited war is impossible. Advocates of the SDI must prove that it is both morally desirable and practical to prepare for limited war. The proposal to plan for limited war is a proposal to reverse the trend of modern warfare. Modern war can be just only if war can be limited, and there is no evidence that it can be.

One can argue convincingly that nations made an understandable but wrong turn in depending on strategic weapons. We have weapons that we are afraid to use, weapons which could destroy our world. A strategic nuclear war would be unjust. A change to a tactical defense would be preferable. All of this can be argued convincingly. However, it does not follow from all of this that we should spend the money and risk upsetting the current strategic balance to make the change to tactical weapons.

Can the SDI Work?

Most discussions of whether the SDI can work center around whether or not it would be technologically possible to build devices that can destroy incoming missiles. Further, these devices must be affordable and must cost less to produce than a potential enemy would spend to build devices that would render them useless. More important than these issues, however, is the issue of whether the SDI can enhance our security.

In the March 23, 1983, speech, President Reagan described the SDI as something that would "give us the means of rendering these weapons impotent and obsolete" and said that the United States would be able to "intercept and destroy strategic ballistic missiles before they could reach our own soil."[27]

What could be wrong with such a system? I would have no objection to such weapons if they could be obtained. The problem is that a total ballistic missile defense system is not possible, and a partial one is extremely dangerous.

The discussion of a total anti-ballistic missile system should remind us of the reasons for accepting a treaty against anti-ballistic missiles. When one side introduces devices for protecting its missiles the other side has a need to build more missiles to insure its ability to retaliate. Unless an anti-ballistic missile system is total, it has the effect of increasing the level of armaments. To avoid an increased arms race the United States and the Soviet Union agreed to allow each other to have ABMs at only one site.

The SDI cannot provide a defense for the United States even if it stopped 90 percent of incoming missiles, which is all its proponents now claim for it. Because it weakens the deterrence power of the other side, the other side would counter it by building more missiles. The SDI would have many consequences, none of which would enhance our security.

Developing tactical weapons will increase the risk of war. That is why both sides agreed to the Anti-Ballistic Missile Treaty. Weapons aimed at weapons, counterforce weapons, would increase the risk of war because each side would have to launch their missiles on warning for fear that their weapons would be knocked out in a first strike, making retaliation impossible. The present counter-population strategy allows each side to wait until their cities are hit before launching their missiles. Each side now knows that if it launched a first strike it would be annihilated by the other side. However, with counterforce weapons a first strike that knocks out the other side might be possible. It then becomes important to hit the other side's weapons before they get yours. Decision time is reduced and reliance on computers is increased.

If the SDI technology worked, it would provide a way of destroying satellites. The same technology that would have to be developed for shooting missiles could easily be used to eliminate satellites. The development of anti-satellite weapons would hurt the United States more than the Soviet Union because the United States is more dependent than the Soviet Union on its satellites. The development of anti-satellite weapons would be disastrous to arms control because both sides rely on their satellites to verify agreements.

If the SDI worked, it would only be effective against missiles entering a country from the upper atmosphere. It would do nothing to stop bombers, missiles from submarines along our coast, or low flying missiles. It reminds me of the line of defenses French Minister of War André Maginot built to make France safe from a German attack before World War II. Just as the Germans went around the Maginot line, an attacker could go around a strategic defense system.

One can consistently admit that having tactical weapons is preferable to having strategic weapons, but that it is not now desirable to try to change the weapons. Developing strategic weapons was wrong. It would have been better to have concentrated on tactical weapons. But the transition at this point would increase the danger of war.

On one side we have the desire to lessen the likelihood of war, and on the other side the desire to lessen the harm if a war does occur. Since I can't know that a war will not occur, why shouldn't we try to save lives by having a system that intercepts as many missiles as possible?

Certainly I believe that we should try to limit the damage of a potential war as much as we can. We can do this without switching to a tactical defense system. All we have to do it to declare regions of each country, and regions of the world, nuclear-free zones. These areas might be opened to inspection from citizens from any country. The choice of which areas are nuclear free, and thus out of the arena of war, could be the subject of negotiations. War would be limited by having no weapons in designated areas.

Making War Just vs. Just Abolishing War

When the suggestion is made that instead of trying to make war more just, we should just abolish war, the rejoinder is made that it is unrealistic to try to abolish war. I believe that the idea of switching now to a tactical defense is far less realistic than the idea of working for enforced international law. This is apparent when we consider the assumptions of SDI.

First, SDI assumes that both sides will switch to a tactical defense system. It simply won't do for only one side to switch its weapon system, as the question of developing neutron bombs illustrates. The neutron bomb, a fusion weapon with little fallout, brings the United States no advantage if the Soviet Union uses fission bombs with large amounts of fallout. If a war occurred the Soviet Union would benefit by having less fallout and damage to its population centers while the United States would be destroyed by large bombs with high levels of fallout.

Unless both sides agree to switch to tactical weapons, there is no incentive for either side to do so—unless it is to prepare for a first strike, in which case the danger of war is increased. To assume that the Soviet Union and the United States are going to come to an agreement to have an orderly switch to tactical weapons is unrealistic, and a switch in weapons makes no sense for the United States unless it is mutual.

In presenting the SDI, President Reagan said that he wanted to share the technology with the Soviet Union. Gorbachev reports that he told Mr. Reagan, "Mr. President, I do not take this idea seriously, your idea about sharing with us the results of research on SDI. You do not even want to share with us oil equipment or equipment for the dairy industry, and still you expect us to believe your promise to share the research developments in the SDI project. That would be something like a 'Second American Revolution,' and revolutions do not occur that often."[28]

In order to have both sides switch to a tactical defense the United States would not only have to share technology, but might also have to build weapons for the Soviet Union if they cannot afford to match us. To think this would occur is totally unrealistic.

Those trying to make war acceptable are too often considered more realistic than those trying to abolish war. Those who want to switch to tactical weapons think that the trend of the past two hundred years toward unlimited war can somehow be reversed. Their view defies the experience of history. It also defies common sense to think that the Soviet Union will not fear a first strike when tactical weapons are in place, or that both sides can negotiate a switch from strategic to tactical weapons.

War must be abolished if humanity is to survive. No just war between nations with nuclear forces is possible. The attempt to make war acceptable only increases the risk of war and puts off the day of its demise. It is as though those who have chosen the military profession are trying to rescue their calling. They realize, like everyone else, that planning for a nuclear Armageddon is wrong. They, like the rest of us, want a change. What they do not see is that the only change left is to abolish war.

Whatever we do—change war or abolish war—will involve a leap into the unknown. Those who advocate a switch to a tactical defense think they can change the rule that nations at war have always used all the force that was available to them. Those who advocate the abolition of war think that they can change the rule that nations have always fought wars. They agree only that the present policy of Mutual Assured Destruction is unacceptable.

The SDI should open a debate on how to best achieve security in the nuclear age, an opportunity that those working for peace should welcome. All parties to this discussion are concerned with the survival of life on the planet. They differ on means, not ends.

The discussion of whether to have counterpopulation weapons or counterforce weapons, MAD or SDI, assumes only two choices. It assumes that we are going to have war and it asks us to judge whether one method is better than the other. Since strategic weapons threaten life on the planet, and tactical weapons offer the hope of limited war and discriminating between combatants and noncombatants, tactical weapons seem morally superior. But there are other issues—whether a transition now to tactical weapons would upset the current strategic balance and increase the risk of war, whether in making war more acceptable we would also make war more likely, whether we should be spending billions to make war more just, or whether we should just abolish war.

Those who criticize the view that war can be abolished and instead want to reform war are on shaky ground. The abolition of war involves applying on a larger scale methods that have been proven to work, for example, the use of courts to settle disputes. There is every reason to believe these methods would work to settle disputes between nations, and no evidence whatsoever for the view that all wars can be limited in the modern age. Those who advocate a switch to tactical weapons cannot cite examples of nations refraining from using their weapons when their national existence is threatened. It defies reason to think that nations will surrender before using their weapons.

Reason favors the abolition of war since military superiority cannot bring political gains in the nuclear age. No longer can any-one benefit from the institution of war. Those who advocate its abolition must enter the discussion of alternatives to the current MAD policy. Instead of wasting our resources trying to make war just, we should just abolish war.

9

■■■

From National Defense to Common Security

■■■

The world is a dangerous place, and we need to find ways to make it less dangerous. I will begin by examining how we got into our current situation and the steps that have been taken to make it less dangerous. Existing treaties attempt to make war more civilized by banning certain types of weapons, keeping areas free of war, and slowing down the arms race. I will also examine alternative proposals to make the world safer, including the proposal to modernize weapons so they are less destructive and the proposal to freeze weapons development. Finally, I will examine some new thinking, including the idea of replacing national defense with common security.

Our Dangerous World

How dangerous is the world today? Today's nuclear arsenals have over one million times the destructive power of the bomb that leveled Hiroshima, which had the destructive power of twelve and a half kilotons of TNT. The average nuclear bomb has a destructive power of two megatons, and there are 50,000 nuclear bombs, each of which could destroy a large city, vaporizing everything within a six-mile radius. Only 3,000 cities on earth have populations of 100,000 or more—the size of Hiroshima—so no cities would remain if even a fraction of the bombs were used.

It is hard to imagine such destructive force. Each of the 50,000 bombs has the explosive force of all the bombs exploded in

World War II. If one took a gymnasium-sized map of the earth (as is done in Buckminster Fuller's Earthgame) and used poker chips to represent accurately each bomb's area of total destruction, it would be readily apparent that even ten thousand bombs would cover the land mass of the earth.

Astronomer Carl Sagan and other scientists estimate that more than 100,000 tons of fine dust would be released into the atmosphere for every megaton exploded.[29] While war planners use 5,000 megatons as a likely amount, Carl Sagan and his colleagues considered a war in which only one hundred megatons was exploded, less than one percent of the arsenal available. The result would be a nuclear winter in which a large cloud blocked the sun and caused subfreezing temperatures for months on end. This nuclear winter would kill all crops, wildlife, and most, if not all, humans.

How did we get into this situation? Once the arms race got started it propelled itself. As soon as one side introduced a weapon the other other side built something to counter it. The reasons one side rather than the other introduced particular weapons have to do with many factors, including technology and geography. The United States had more to gain in developing submarine technology because of its many warm weather ports, while the Soviet Union had more interest in developing intercontinental ballistic missiles because it lacked air bases near the United States. Because both sides try to develop weapons as quickly as they can, coming in second reflects a difference in technological level, not in moral values.

There are several lessons that can be learned from the history of the arms race. Whenever one side introduces a new weapon, the other side is sure to follow. Introducing a new weapon brings no long-term advantage because the other side soon develops that weapon. Both sides end up losing because both spend more money on armaments and become less secure.

Agreements to Control Dangers

Many agreements have tried to make the world less dangerous, some bilateral and some multilateral, signed by nations that promise to adhere to them. The number of nations signing varies, and parties who do not sign cannot be forced to follow the treaties.

Several treaties ban the use of particular weapons in the conduct of war. The use of poison gas was banned in 1925 in the Protocol for the Prohibition of Asphyxiating, Poisonous or Other

Gases, and of Bacteriological Methods of Warfare, a treaty prompted by the 1.3 million casualties of poison gas in World War I,
including 100,000 fatalities. The treaty, signed by 110 nations as of
July 1988, neither forbids the development, production, stockpiling, or deployment of chemical or biological weapons nor provides
procedures for handling violations. It is widely believed that chemical weapons were used in the Iran-Iraq war and plants for making
chemical weapons are being built in Third World countries. Unlike
the poison gas treaty, the 1972 Prohibition of the Development,
Production and Stockpiling of Bacteriological (Biological) and
Toxin Weapons and on Their Destruction mandated the actual
destruction of biological weapons, the first multilateral agreement
to provide a measure of disarmament. As of July 1988, it has 109
parties. A treaty forbidding the Hostile Use of Environmental
Modification Techniques bans the manipulation of nature to cause
earthquakes, tidal waves, or flooding, and the Inhumane Weapons
Convention restricts the use of mines, booby traps, incendiary
weapons, and fragmentation weapons.

Several treaties have as their aim keeping areas free of
weapons. A 1971 treaty prohibits placing nuclear weapons on the
sea bed and the ocean floor farther than twelve miles from the
coast, and a 1979 treaty bans the use of the moon and planets for
military purposes. The Antarctic region was demilitarized in a
1959 treaty. Regional agreements to prevent nuclear arms races
include a 1967 Prohibition of Nuclear Weapons in Latin America
and a 1985 treaty establishing a South Pacific Nuclear Free Zone.
The nuclear powers that signed the 1968 Treaty on the Non-
Proliferation of Nuclear Weapons agreed to refrain from helping
non-nuclear nations get the bomb, to negotiate in good faith to
cease all testing of nuclear weapons, and to seek both a cessation of
the arms race and nuclear disarmament.

The United States and the Soviet Union have several agreements designed to reduce the risk of accidental war. A 1963 Mem-
orandum of Understanding established a direct communications
link between Moscow and Washington, commonly called the hot
line. The 1971 Agreement on Measures to Reduce the Risk of
Outbreak of Nuclear War included the provision that each side
must notify the other of experimental launchings beyond national
boundaries. A 1987 Agreement on the Establishment of Nuclear
Risk Reduction Centers established centers in Washington and

Moscow, and the following year an Agreement on Notification of Launches stipulated that each side must use the centers to notify the other party when launching any intercontinental or submarine-launched ballistic missile.

Recent Treaties and Current Talks

Several recent treaties limit the arms race and one actually reduces the number of weapons. As a result of the first round of Strategic Arms Limitation Talks (SALT 1, 1972), a five-year interim agreement set limits on the total number of launchers for fixed land-based intercontinental ballistic missiles (ICBMs) and of ballistic missile launchers on submarines. On its expiration in 1977, both sides indicated that they would abide by its limits while seeking another agreement. A second round of talks (SALT 2, 1986) limited each side to a total of 2,250 missiles after 1981 and included detailed limits on numbers, testing, deployment, modification, replacement, and conversion of particular weapons systems. It also set limits on the number of warheads per missile. This treaty was not ratified by the U.S. Senate, and since 1984 each side has claimed that the other has violated the treaty.

The only treaty that has led to the destruction of nuclear weapons is the 1987 Treaty on the Elimination of Intermediate-Range and Shorter-Range Missiles, known as the INF Treaty. It eliminates an entire class of weapons—all the parties' ground-launched intermediate range and shorter-range missiles and the launchers of such missiles. The treaty includes verification by on-site inspection in addition to satellite observation and established a special verification commission to resolve questions related to compliance. The current Strategic Arms Reduction Talks (START), like the INF Treaty, aim at reducing the number of weapons. An impasse in these talks was broken when Premier Gorbachev asked, "How about if we split the difference?" and Secretary of State James Baker replied, "You've got a deal."[30] Each side would set a limit of 880 sea-launched missiles and limit the range of air-launched missiles to 375 miles. Progress on this treaty has been held up because of differences on the SDI.

The United States and the Soviet Union both want an agreement that each side destroy 80 percent of its stockpile of chemical weapons within eight years, during which time they would try to attain a global ban on chemical weapons. They would then destroy the remaining 20 percent, completing the entire process of removing chemical weapons within ten years. Progress on banning chemical weapons will depend on attaining the agreement of other countries, including Libya and Iraq, to ban these weapons, countries who may not agree to a ban of the "poor nations' weapons" without a ban of nuclear weapons.

Before the collapse of communism and the resulting independence of most states within the Warsaw bloc, the United States and the Soviet Union had discussed halving their troops in Europe; now the Soviet Union has been forced by events to withdraw its troops.

Although these agreements provide hope for the future, they do not substantially reduce the number of weapons in the world. Even if the proposed START agreement goes into effect, the world will have as many nuclear warheads in the year 2000 as it had in 1980, still over a million times the force that destroyed Hiroshima. The INF Treaty was easier to obtain than future steps will be, because it eliminated an entire class of weapons and thus did not involve verifying the number of weapons that remain. Finally, new agreements, as well as compliance with several old agreements, will be considered in terms of the SDI.

Treaties Relevant to the SDI

Several treaties are relevant to the SDI. The 1967 Treaty Governing the Activities of States in the Exploration and Use of Outer Space prohibits placing nuclear or other weapons of mass destruction in earth orbit and on the planets, or stationing them in outer space. One version of the SDI would involve having nuclear-powered laser weapons in orbit around the earth.

The United States and the Soviet Union are currently discussing the possibility of banning all testing of nuclear weapons. In 1963 the Treaty Banning Nuclear Weapons Tests in the Atmosphere, in Outer Space and Underwater banned tests everywhere but under the ground. In 1974 the test ban treaty was expanded to rule out tests with a yield of more than 150 kilotons, which still allows the development of low-yield weapons. Some versions of the SDI would use low-yield nuclear weapons and the United States has been testing such weapons. The Comprehensive Test Ban Treaty, like many other treaties, is tied up with the issue of continuing with the SDI.

The treaty most relevant to the SDI, indeed the treaty that the Soviet Union believes prohibits SDI, is the 1972 Treaty on the Limitation of Anti-Ballistic Missile Systems. Before this treaty, the Soviet Union had deployed anti-ballistic missile systems at two sites to provide a defense against strategic weapons. At that time the United States sought and achieved a ban on strategic defense systems. In the ABM Treaty, negotiated in the first stage of the SALT talks (1969–72), the United States and the Soviet Union agreed not to develop, test, or deploy ABM systems or components that are air-based, space-based, or mobile land-based. Each side was allowed to have two ABM sites in its country, limited to one hundred missiles each. The Soviet Union retained only its system around Moscow and the United States decided not to build any ABM system. In anticipation of new technologies such as laser weapons, the parties agreed that in the event ABM systems based on physical principles other than missiles become possible, limitations on such systems would be subject to discussion under articles of the treaty. The treaty established a consultative commission to consider questions regarding compliance.

Perhaps the most important meeting on arms control was that between Premier Gorbachev and President Reagan in Reykjavik, Iceland, in 1986, at which the discussion showed clearly the relationship between the ABM Treaty, SDI, and the reduction or elimination of strategic weapons.

Gorbachev suggested a 50 percent reduction of strategic arms, "with a view to fully eliminating these deadliest of weapons by the end of the century." Another agreement he advocated would state, "The sides should strengthen the ABM Treaty . . . by assuming equal commitments not to use the right to pull out of the Treaty within the ten year period." Gorbachev argued that the ABM Treaty would have to be strengthened before strategic weapons could be reduced: "Since we are entering a totally new situation which will witness the beginning of substantial reductions in nuclear weapons and their complete elimination in the foreseeable future, it is necessary to protect oneself from any unexpected developments. We are speaking of weapons which to this day make up the core of this country's defenses. Therefore, it is necessary to exclude everything that could undermine equality in the process of disarmament, to preclude any chance of developing weapons of a new type which would ensure military superiority." Gorbachev claimed, "We have now been convinced one more time that the

U.S. Administration, confident in American technological superiority, is hoping to obtain military superiority through SDI. And so it has gone so far as to bury the accords which had almost been achieved and on which we already reached agreement."[31]

The SDI: American and Soviet Positions

None of the positions on the arms race can properly be thought of as American or Soviet positions. Although the Soviet Union was the first to want a strategic defense system, and the United States was the first to propose a nuclear freeze, both have switched their views on these issues. Rather than think of proposals as American or Soviet, it is better to think of the nuclear arms race as a problem that bothers both sides, with people on both sides trying to figure out what to do.

Throughout the 1960s, the Soviet Union wanted both sides to be able to have anti-ballistic missile systems and the United States insisted that anti-ballistic missiles be banned, an insistence than resulted in the Anti-Ballistic Missile Treaty of 1972 that strictly limited anti-missile defense. The United States advocated the view that the best way to avoid war was for each side's population to be exposed to the other in a policy of Mutual Assured Destruction (MAD). Now the United States wants to give up the policy of Mutual Assured Destruction for anti-missile defense systems.

The SDI is hindering progress on arms control. Because it requires new missiles and smaller nuclear warheads, proceeding with this system means developing new missiles, continuing to test nuclear weapons, and placing weapons in space.

The SDI would start another arms race. Because SDI could not stop all missiles, it is now being suggested as a method for enhancing deterrence by insuring that the country that is attacked will still have missiles to retaliate. However, if SDI enhances the ability of one nation to withstand an attack, it weakens the power of the other to retaliate. So a nation that wants to insure that it would have enough weapons to destroy the other after it is attacked would have to build more weapons to overcome the attacker's strategic defense system.

A nation that wants to develop a strategic defense system does not want limitations on the development of new missiles, new atomic bombs, or new weapons for space. A nation that fears a first strike by a country that has a strategic defense system does not want limits on the number of missiles it can launch in retaliation for a first strike. The development of a strategic defense system will have a devastating effect on arms control.

Nuclear Freeze

A nuclear freeze is not a new idea. President Lyndon Johnson put forth a proposal for a Soviet-American freeze on the "number and character of strategic and defensive vehicles" in January 1964 (a proposal prepared by President Kennedy, who had directed his arms control negotiators to come up with a freeze proposal in 1963). At the time, the United States had 7,000 strategic nuclear warheads, 1,100 strategic missiles, and over 1,000 strategic bombers. The Soviet Union had less than one-fiftieth as many weapons. The Soviets rejected a freeze almost immediately because they did not want to have their forces frozen into a position of permanent inferiority.

In 1970, a comprehensive freeze on offensive and defensive weapons received a vote of seventy-three to six in the U.S. Senate. President Nixon refused to pursue the idea of a comprehensive freeze. Instead, he and National Security Adviser Henry Kissinger held talks in Moscow in 1972 that culminated in SALT I and the Anti-Ballistic Missile Treaty.

Supporters of a nuclear freeze have backed legislation such as the Kennedy-Hatfield Congressional Resolution, which states: "As an immediate strategic arms control objective, the United States and the Soviet Union should: (a) pursue a complete halt to the nuclear arms race; (b) decide when and how to achieve a mutual and verifiable freeze on the testing, production, and future deployment of nuclear warheads, missiles, and other delivery systems; and (c) give special attention to destabilizing weapons whose deployment would make a freeze more difficult to achieve."[32]

It is interesting that the United States proposed a freeze to the Soviet Union when the United States had a fifty-to-one advantage in weapons, and later under President Reagan refused to support a freeze when both sides are roughly equal. If it was fair to expect the Soviet Union to freeze their weapons at one-fiftieth the level of U.S. weapons, then it is fair to expect Americans to accept a level close to parity.

Because the United States and the Soviet Union are roughly equal in weapons, now is the time for a freeze. (I say "roughly equal" because there is no foolproof way to compare different weapons systems. It isn't clear how to count the greater megatonnage of one side or the greater accuracy of the other, or whether we should count British and French weapons.) If a freeze is not enacted, the next generation of weapons is going to change the nature of the arms race and make a nuclear war more likely.

The choice of peace versus war has always been a choice of whether governments will try to dominate others or learn to live and let live. To refuse to accept a freeze sends the message that we hope to achieve a technological advantage that will allow us to dominate others. To accept a freeze is to say that we will give up our hope of domination.

People decide to forego their hope of dominating others by the following reasoning. Each side naturally wants to dominate the other, because each gets the greatest rewards by dominating others. While being in the situation of the dominant party is the most desirable outcome for each side, it is not possible for both sides to dominate; nor is it likely that one side will always dominate. The most likely outcome is that both sides will end up fighting for the dominant position, an outcome desirable for neither side. Compared to the continuation of an arms race, or to an all-out nuclear exchange, having both sides give up the hope of achieving dominance is the most desirable outcome.

It does not matter whether one side is slightly ahead in armaments. The two sides are more equal now than ever before, development of new weapons at this time would increase rather than decrease the chance of war, and neither side presently has the capacity to dominate the other. A nuclear freeze would send the message that each side is giving up the hope of dominating the other and seeking ways to live at peace.

The nuclear freeze idea has problems, but whatever we do at this point in the arms race will involve problems. Advocacy of a freeze should not be thought of as advocacy of the current policy of Mutual Assured Destruction, nor should it be thought of as freezing us into the current level of armaments.

Common Security

Too often a discussion of the issues of war and peace centers only on the number of missiles each side has and other quantitative questions. The use of numbers can mislead if it gives credence to assumptions that should be questioned. More and more people are starting to question the entire concept of national defense and want to replace it with a concept of common security.

The concept of common security was much in evidence at the recent Third Special Session on Disarmament. "More than ever before, nations were adopting a holistic perspective, viewing disarmament as part of a broader, common concern for security which must be equally guaranteed to all nations. The role of the United Nations was stressed to a greater degree. Clearly, there was a movement away from "weaponitis" (focusing solely on excessive stockpiles of national weaponry—especially nuclear weapons) to an expanded concept of common security which goes beyond disarmament."[33]

Common security includes many ideas. It involves renouncing the use of military force as an instrument for resolving disputes between nations and renouncing the view that security can be attained through military superiority. Following this concept, nations must give up the attempt to seek advantages through the use of military power. The basic notion of common security, that one nation cannot be secure unless other nations are also secure, contrasts with the national defense view that nations can attain security by increasing their military strength.

Common security assumes that we will learn to live together or we will die together, an assumption reflected in the Anti-Ballistic Missile Treaty: "Each party undertakes not to deploy ABM systems for defense of the territory of its country and not to provide a base for such defense." Advocates of national defense would like the United States to try to build a system to defend us against nuclear attack, while advocates of common security want all of us to recognize that we will either all survive or all perish. Upon that recognition, alternatives to war will be sought.

Part IV

From Enemies to Friends

'I JUST KEPT PECKING AT IT.'

■ I was angry with my friend:
I told my wrath, my wrath did end.
I was angry with my foe:
I told it not, my wrath did grow.
—William Blake

10

■ ■ ■

Why the U.S. and the USSR Need Common Security

■ ■ ■

Tremendous change has occurred in the Soviet Union and Eastern Europe and there is potential for more positive change. We need to make sure that we don't take actions that preclude the possibility of desirable change. In this chapter I examine the changes and the choices that will determine how far the changes can go, including troop reductions in Europe and the independence of the Baltic states. In chapter 11, I show how changes in the Soviet Union have affected people in one city, Krasnodar, and how American citizen diplomats can aid the process of change. In chapter 12, I examine how far a process of honest interchange might go, as I report on a discussion between philosophers in the United States and the Soviet Union on questions that divide the two countries.

Sometimes when problems cannot be solved within the existing framework, the only solution is to change the framework. Given the two hostile blocs in Europe, NATO and the Warsaw Pact and the nation-state system of security, the Soviet Union has apprehensions now that a unified Germany is part of NATO and fears granting the Baltic states independence. However, given a system of security under an expanded European Community and worldwide enforcement of international law, the independence of the Baltic states poses no danger. The Soviet Union thus has a strong incentive to have a new system of security.

The United States also has a strong incentive for change. Its budget deficit of $3 trillion will be impossible to pay off if the country continues current spending on defense. A different system of security—common security—would allow the United States to reduce its spending and even to sell resources such as land and buildings used by the military. Conventional arms limitation in Europe and further reductions in armaments depend on establishing alternative security arrangements.

The Changes in the Eastern Bloc

"Better dead than Red" was the motto of many U.S. conservatives in the 1950s, who assumed that once a nation became Communist, it lost its freedom forever.

Country after country rejected communism during 1989, a process that began with the ascension of Mikhail S. Gorbachev to power. In 1986 the Communist party gave more power to local parliaments and in 1987 held multicandidate elections to those parliaments. A special party conference in 1988 promised to shift power from the party to the government, and Gorbachev suggested that local party leaders should have to win election to government posts. Constitutional amendments were proposed to change the national parliament from a rubber stamp to a real legislature and to have multicandidate elections for that body. In 1989 the Soviet Union had its first multicandidate elections for parliament, and dozens of Communist leaders were defeated. The First Congress of People's Deputies opened. The Soviet Union's first parliamentary opposition, the Inter-Regional Group, formed. Lithuania approved a multiparty system and Lithuanian Communists voted to become an independent party. In 1990, Gorbachev dropped his opposition to a multiparty system. Hundreds of thousands marched through Moscow to demand democratic reform. On February 7, 1990, members of the Central Committee agreed to abolish the party's constitutional guarantee of power.

Within a span of five years the Soviet Union went from a dictatorship where the Communist party had a guaranteed monopoly on power to almost a democratic society. While this pace of change is staggering, the changes in Eastern Europe occurred even more quickly. During one year, 1989, the Communist governments of Hungary, Czechoslovakia, Poland, and East Germany all fell, and the government in Rumania shortly after.

The first independent trade union in the Soviet bloc, Solidarity, led the movement for change when a series of talks between the union and the Polish government led to an agreement to hold free elections. Solidarity swept the Eastern Bloc's first free elections in forty years. Meanwhile Hungary opened its borders with Austria, the Berlin Wall was torn down, and plans were under way for free elections in Hungary, Czechoslovakia, and East Germany. Communists lost in all the elections. Rumania experienced a violent upheaval and another Communist government fell. By 1990 nothing remained of the governments that Stalin had installed after World War II.

Many of these changes were instituted by people who had called themselves Communists. The Communist party of Hungary discarded Communism and calls itself the Socialist party. Just as most Communists in the West lost their faith in communism after Stalin came to power, so individuals in the Eastern Bloc now lost their faith. It took them longer because their governments isolated them from news of the outside world and from their own history. Eventually modern communications and visitors from outside ended that isolation.

How far the process of change will go in the Soviet Union and Eastern Europe will depend in part on what the United States does. A Soviet Union that feels threatened will fight the independence movements in the Baltic states and will again be prone to a military dictatorship.

Alliances vs. Common Security

There are two approaches nations can take today in seeking national security. A nation can join with other nations in an alliance or can, together with other nations, establish a system of collective security. The United States at first resisted and then joined alliances. George Washington warned against such a move because he feared such alliances would drag the United States into wars. After World War I, President Wilson tried to establish a system of collective security with the League of Nations. He conceived of a common security system as a replacement for the failed alliances that existed before the war. We might consider today's alliances a replacement for the non-working United Nations common security system. Today, we have a choice between continuing to rely on alliances with NATO and the Warsaw Pact or trying to establish a workable system of common security.

Good reasons lay behind establishing the NATO alliance. Fear of the Russians was not irrational. Stalin did make a deal with Hitler to divide Poland, he did keep his troops in Eastern Europe after the war, and it is only now that Poland has finally gained her independence. In a real sense World War II has not ended until now for the millions of people in Eastern Europe who lost their independence to Hitler and Stalin, and then to Stalin's heirs. With the end of Soviet domination of Eastern Europe, a new era has begun.

The causes of the cold war no longer exist. New ideas are needed. The old idea was that two blocs of nations, the NATO alliance and the Warsaw Pact, would balance each other in Europe. Now, with many Warsaw Pact nations no longer Communist and Germany united, it does not make sense to think in terms of hostile alliances.

The Soviet Union and Common Security

How do we fit newly united Germany into the alliance system? Does former East Germany simply go from one side to the other, so that NATO gains, and the Warsaw Pact loses? Since no one wants to be a loser, the Soviet Union will rightfully be concerned with a hostile alliance facing it that includes a unified Germany. If we want the process of change to continue in the Eastern Bloc, including progress on the independence of the Baltic states, a way must be found to make the Soviet Union feel more secure. The solution is to fit Germany into a new common security system for Europe, not into an alliance, which means that the European Community must move more quickly than planned to establish such a system.

Gorbachev envisions an expanded European Community. A unified Germany can fit within this community and not be a threat to the Soviet Union because this community would work on the doctrine of common security and not national defense—Germany would not have military forces powerful enough to threaten the Soviet Union. Independent Baltic states, and even the Soviet Union itself, could fit within such a community. Having a united Germany and independent Baltic states join NATO is not acceptable to the Soviet Union.

The pieces of a new positive order are almost, though not quite, in place. Whether the change process continues in the Soviet Union and Eastern Europe, whether progress in reducing conventional arms in Europe continues, and whether progress will continue in controlling nuclear arms now depend on establishing common security in Europe.

Mikhail Gorbachev speaks of "a common European house." Francois Mitterrand, president of France, speaks of a "broad confederation." Both seek a new Europe to replace the arrangements made at Yalta and Potsdam after World War II. At present there are twelve nations in the European Community and thirty-five in the Conference on Security and Cooperation in Europe (CSCE) which has become an important forum for discussing the shape of a new Europe.

The CSCE, also known as the Helsinki process, includes every nation in Europe except Albania, the United States, Canada, and the Soviet Union. It was founded in the 1975 Helsinki Final Act which, in addition to stating human rights, provided guidelines for East-West cooperation in security. For ten years the Helsinki process was known only for human rights, with little action on security matters. After Gorbachev came to power in 1985, the CSCE became a useful forum for talks on arms control and confidence-building measures such as prior notification of military maneuvers. One advantage of the CSCE is that nations can express their views as individual nations and not as members of military blocs. Also, because the CSCE includes both the United States and the Soviet Union, it would be possible for both these nations to keep troops in Europe as copeacekeepers in a new Europe, rather than as the heads of opposing blocs. It is even conceivable that United States and Soviet troops in Europe could be under the command of the CSCE.

A unified Germany within a common European system of security is a threat to no nation. A unified Germany under no restraints is unacceptable to many nations, including the Soviet Union, France, and Poland. Germans understand this and many members of the German Social Democratic party support replacing the existing military pacts with an all-European security system.

One issue facing the European Community is whether to include the new East European nations. Jacques Delors, the head of the community, wants to create what he calls "three concentric circles." The first includes the twelve nations already in the European Community. The second includes the six nations that form the European Free Trade Association—Switzerland, Sweden, Norway, Finland, Iceland, and Austria. The third includes the newly independent Eastern European countries together with countries on Europe's outer fringes including Turkey, Malta, and Cyprus.[1] The French might want the Soviet Union and the nations of Eastern Europe to be part of the European community to balance the tremendous economic power of a unified Germany.

One system of common security might be established for Europe and another for all nations through the United Nations. In 1987, Gorbachev proposed a comprehensive system of international security with a central role for the United Nations in conflict resolution. He advocated increasing the use of UN military observers and peacekeeping forces to disengage warring parties in regional conflicts. Action followed as the Soviet Union cooperated with UN observers in Afghanistan and supported UN peacekeepers in Iran and Iraq and UN observers in Namibia. Gorbachev's proposal for using the permanent members of the Security Council as guarantors of regional security was embodied in General Assembly Resolution 42/93 which called for a Comprehensive System of International Peace and Security.

The United States and the Soviet Union cosponsored a 1989 UN resolution on peace, security and international cooperation. A November 3, 1989, press release from the U.S. mission to the United Nations noted, "Perhaps the most important thing about this resolution is not its specific language, but what it symbolizes as a new beginning at the United Nations—a new spirit of constructive cooperation."

The United States and the Soviet Union can work together to strengthen common security through the United Nations. The United States can support common security in Europe to replace the system of alliances. A new approach might allow the United States to solve its budget deficit problems, and only new security arrangements in Europe will allay the Soviet Union's fear of a unified Germany. New approaches are imperative if the process of change is to continue in the Soviet Union. Those changes have opened up new possibilities—possibilities that we must now either grasp or lose.

The United States and Common Security

The national debt, tripled during President Reagan's term of office, is now more than $3 trillion and still rising. President Reagan accrued more debt than all previous presidents combined, mostly as a result of military spending. In 1988 the United States spent more on the military and on debt payments due to previous military spending ($504 billion) than it collected from all corporate and income taxes ($499 billion). The cold war military expenditures have threatened the economic future of the United States.

Because of past and present military expenditures, money is not available to handle crises the United States must face. The failure of over a thousand savings and loan institutions during the Reagan years will cost over $500 billion. The Farmer's Home Administration has a $22 billion deficit and will require a taxpayer-financed bailout. The Federal Pension Benefit Guaranty Corporation is running a $45 billion deficit and will have to be bailed out or more than 40 million Americans won't get pensions. Meanwhile the infrastructure rots, more than a quarter of U.S. students drop out of high school, and the use of drugs increases.

U.S. taxpayers now have to pay off a $3 trillion debt, about $15,000 for each man, woman, and child in the United States. The interest alone is over $1,000 a year for each person. This debt load gives the United States a strong incentive to seek another means of security besides military alliances.

The overwhelming national debt is causing many undesirable changes in the United States. The debt is owned largely by foreigners who will more and more be able to influence our national policies, just as the United States dictates policies to countries that owe it money. The United States demands that its debtors institute austerity programs and can expect its creditors to do likewise. Already domestic spending cuts have reduced many essential programs and will end up costing more than the programs would have cost. Nutritional programs for children that have been cut would prevent more expensive medical problems. Road repair has been put off, which will cost much more later. As people in the United States continue to experience a decline in their life-style they will demand alternatives.

The country does not have to continue spending money on

national defense but could, together with the Soviet Union, establish a system of common security. A start can be made in Europe where the ingredients are almost in place and the need is urgent. In addition to regional common security arrangements, such as in Europe, the United Nations and international law could be jointly strengthened. U.S. expenditures on the military each year equal the amount of U.S. deficits. Without military expenditures the budget could be balanced. Once a system of common security was in place, military bases would be obsolete. Land and buildings used for military purposes could be sold to pay off the national debt.

We cannot solve the world's environment and energy problems as long as the world's resources keep going for armaments. The environmental crisis, caused largely by the burning of fossil fuels, can be solved if we have the resources to do what is necessary. We can invest in a change from fossil fuels to solar energy. Silicon cells can produce electricity that can be conducted through tanks of sea water to produce hydrogen gas to power our automobiles and factories. Once in place we would have almost free energy that causes no pollution, but the initial costs are large. Investing in solar energy would simultaneously reduce the greenhouse effect and provide an alternative to the fossil fuels that are being depleted.

Possibilities that were once dreams are now realistic. In 1940, Clarence K. Streit dreamed of a union of democracies.[2] He and the thousands of people in his organization believed that it would be possible to make a start towards world government with a union of democratic nations, and then have other nations join the union. One problem with the United Nations is that many member nations have been dictatorships and totalitarian regimes. Now we can envision the European Community as a union of democracies that other nations might join as they embrace democracy and we can even envision the United Nations as someday being a union of democracies.

11

■■■

American Soviet Citizen Diplomacy

■■■

As the founder of a sister city program between Tallahassee, Florida, and Krasnodar in the Soviet Union, I have witnessed the changes in the Soviet Union from 1984 to the present. When I presented our Sister City Resolution to the Tallahassee City Commission in 1984, one person spoke against the resolution. He argued that citizen diplomacy could not work with the Soviet Union because their society was centrally controlled. The speaker was right. Although after 1985 changes occurred quickly, it took four years and the coming to power of Mikhail Gorbachev before the city of Krasnodar accepted our invitation. Today, Friends of Tallahassee in Krasnodar, completely separate from any government or Communist control, has five hundred members. They have a "Tallahassee Street" and want Tallahassee businesses involved in their city. Ordinary citizens of Krasnodar have come to our city and we have had yearly trips of delegates from Tallahassee visiting Krasnodar, engaging in an honest exchange of viewpoints.

The ideal change in American/Soviet relations would be to transform ourselves from enemies to friends. Real friends go out of their way to avoid hurting each other—they are sensitive to each other's feelings and needs. Being friends doesn't mean agreeing on everything, but when a friendship is important, people restrain their behavior to protect it.

Before friendship can develop, people must first communicate. Anything that increases communication between American and Soviet citizens serves the cause of peace, because when people talk they tend to come closer together in their views. The process can start with something as simple as exchanges in music, athletics, and education. Once people are comfortable, they will start to discuss the issues that divide them. Through their discussions they will learn the merits of each other's viewpoints and either agree or respect each other for their differences.

Establishing a Sister City Relationship

The easiest way to start a sister city program is to contact people who already have a program and invite a citizen diplomat to speak in your city. My wife and I heard of a sister city program in Gainesville, Florida, and we invited representatives of their group to give a public talk in Tallahassee. We booked the meeting room of a local bank for a talk by Steven and Natasha Kalishman on the topic "Starting A Sister City Program."

Steve and Natasha met while he was working in the merchant marine, delivering grain to the Soviet Union. While on leave from his ship, he took a tour and Natasha was his tour guide. Although they live in Gainesville, Natasha has kept her Soviet citizenship, which makes it easier for her to visit her parents in the Soviet Union. Before one of their visits to her mother, a friend suggested that they carry a resolution from the city of Gainesville inviting her hometown of Novorossiisk to be a sister city. They delivered that resolution and the following year led a delegation of Gainesville citizens to Novorossiisk. After hearing the report on how well the Gainesville resolution and citizen diplomats had been received, fifteen individuals volunteered to serve on a board of directors of our Tallahassee group.

Our newly formed sister city organization conducted a careful campaign to insure that our city would pass a resolution inviting Krasnodar to be our sister city. We approached each member of our city commission twice, first with a draft of the resolution and then with changes commission members requested.

On July 17, 1984, I presented our resolution to the Tallahassee City Commission as the representative of the Tallahassee Krasnodar Sister City Program. In my talk I explained that Krasnodar is located one hour from the Black Sea and that, like Tallahassee, it is the capital of its region. The resolution passed unanimously. Two residents of Tallahassee, Mark and Sandra Greenfield, were designated by the city commission to carry to the city of Krasnodar the resolution, which stated:

> The City of Tallahassee, Florida, USA, desires to . . . invite the City of Krasnodar, Russian Federated Republic, to become its Sister City so that people of both cities will be able to communicate with one another and share the attainment of these common goals: namely, the development of mutual friendships and a better understanding of each other's civilization through cultural, athletic and educational exchanges.
>
> Be it resolved, therefore, that the Mayor, the City Commission, and the Citizens of Tallahassee hereby invite the City of Krasnodar to be associated with the said City of Tallahassee as a "Sister City" in order to promote and carry out these exchanges between the citizens of the respective cities to the betterment of all concerned.

The Greenfields presented the resolution to the mayor of Krasnodar, along with letters of friendship from local universities, the school board, and local civic and religious organizations. They were warmly received and were told that the resolution would have to be taken to their town council for approval.

The Greenfields were able to begin one exchange program immediately. As a result of their visit, the Tallahassee-Krasnodar Sister City Program has had yearly exchanges of children's art. Children at all public schools in Leon County participate, with one work from each school selected. Before they are sent to the Soviet Union, the works are displayed at Tallahassee City Hall and the artists receive certificates from the mayor.

Changes in the Soviet Union

In 1987, my wife and I made a trip to Krasnodar as delegates of our sister city program. I also read a paper at an International Philosophy of Science meeting at Moscow State University, and we visited refuseniks, people who had been refused the right to leave the Soviet Union. We witnessed some changes in the Soviet Union and were able to learn what Soviet citizens thought of them.

Ours was the fourth delegation from Tallahassee, and Krasnodar still had not responded to our invitation to become sister cities. Before the trip each of the twelve delegation members listed the groups and sorts of people they wanted to meet. We all wanted to make contacts with ordinary Soviet citizens.

It would be easy to visit the Soviet Union and learn little about the social situation. The Intourist agency, which has a monopoly on providing tour guides, can keep travelers busy all day seeing tourist sites and never meeting ordinary people. One evening when we had planned to mingle with Soviet citizens at a theater production, we were taken to a hotel exclusively for English-speaking people—even the signs on the rest rooms were in English. The only way to see what the Soviet Union is really like is to go off on your own while the rest of your group does its touring, and to insist on meetings with people you choose.

I had asked to meet with the Krasnodar Peace Committee and with a fellow philosopher. The city of Krasnodar had chosen Professor Boris Kibonski for my counterpart meeting, but, unfortunately, both meetings were scheduled for the same time. Our translator explained that there were not enough people to meet with the peace committee and asked if we would accompany Judy Felder and Tallahassee peace activist Ed Green to that meeting.

There, a spokeswoman explained the history of their group and described their activities in aiding the victims of natural disasters, providing funds to foreign students, building monuments to those who died in World War II, and demonstrating for nuclear disarmament. Ed Green of the Tallahassee Peace Coalition showed the group an album he had compiled of activities for both peace and justice that occur in Tallahassee, including information on the coalition and local groups opposed to apartheid. Judy Felder spoke of attempts by social workers and educators to redirect money being spent on armaments to meet human needs. Then, as agreed, we began a discussion of approaches to peace.

I presented the view that we should strengthen the United Nations and have enforced international law so that decisions of the World Court, such as the decision that the United States should stop supporting the Contras in Nicaragua, must be obeyed. Everyone clapped. When I added that I favored enforcement of the decisions of the UN General Assembly, such as the almost unanimous UN declaration for the withdrawal of Soviet troops from Afganistan, there was less applause, but among those clapping was one respectable-looking gentleman in the Krasnodar Peace Committee.

When it came time for questions from the audience, a young man stated that he had heard of a U.S. citizen who was unable to get medical care for lack of money. He asked me to confirm that in the United States you had to have money to get medical care. Rather than let this fellow score points in front of Communist party officials I answered that citizens in the United States do not have a right to medical care, as they do in the Soviet Union. Citizens in each country have a different set of rights. In the United States any citizen has the right to own a printing press and to publish whatever he or she wants.

The same man asked, "Can you really publish whatever you want?" I showed him a short pamphlet I had brought entitled "Thinking About Peace," and told him that I had produced the master of this pamphlet myself using a personal computer and had it printed at a local print shop. I also showed him a book entitled "The Best Investment: Land in a Loving Community,"[3] which I self-published. He was amazed that Americans had the right to publish whatever they wanted.

We had a wide-ranging discussion of rights, comparing the rights that Soviet citizens have to medical care and housing with the rights that Americans have to express themselves freely and elect their leaders. Philosopher Boris Kibonski then made a comment. "I want all the rights that Dr. Felder has mentioned and more besides. I want an entire rainbow of rights."

After the formal part of the meeting with the Krasnodar Peace Committee, an architect by the name of Yuri Subbotin approached us with a painting in his hands. He said that he painted in his spare time and that he wanted us to have a painting he called "Autumn Fire," his vision of the world on fire from a nuclear war. Mr. Subbotin spoke from his heart when he told me that he thought working for peace should be our top priority.

My impression of the Krasnodar Peace Committee is that like individuals in our peace organizations, many of its members are sincerely concerned about world peace. Some Communist party officials act as the spokespersons of their peace group. When Ed Green asked about the decision-making process of the peace committee and whether individuals can decide on the activities of the organization, his question was ignored.

We confronted them openly with our concerns. We said we had started the exchange program because we wanted exchanges of ordinary citizens, not just government bureaucrats. They assured us that they also wanted exchanges with ordinary citizens. It was their practice, they said, to balance the groups they send so that at least 30 percent are workers, and there is a balance between professions. They said they would not want to just send Communist party members and politicians. We told them that we were uncomfortable dealing with a government group, and that we wish that their sister city group, like ours, was a nongovernment group. Finally, we said that we were disappointed that their city had not yet accepted our invitation, that we would give them no more than one year to accept our invitation, and that we would then find another city for a sister city relationship.

Within a year Krasnodar accepted a sister city relationship with us and also established a nongovernment Friends of Tallahassee organization. One hundred and fifty members of this society met our next delegation. This nongovernment organization has spawned several equally independent clubs for exchanges. A press club initiated a "press-bridge" that involved our writing articles for each other's newspapers, which appear uncensored. The Russian Orthodox clergy have established contact with Greek Orthodox and other Christian churches in Tallahassee. Doctors, engineers, teachers, radio engineers, and athletes have also established clubs. The business club has proposed setting up a joint broiler factory and a pig farm and wants to explore other ideas for joint enterprises. Women's groups in Tallahassee now have counterparts in the women's club offshoot of the Friends of Tallahassee and a club for nature conservation is in contact with our environmental groups.

In 1990 the sister city program hosted a medical delegation from Krasnodar consisting of six doctors who spent eight weeks studying cardiovascular techniques and procedures at the Tallahassee Regional Medical Center. Prior to their visit no physicians or facilities in the Krasnodar region provided the lifesaving techniques the doctors were able to learn in Tallahassee.

The exchange of delegations has changed people. After my neighbor Ron Campbell read in the paper that a visiting citizen of Krasnodar was an avid fisherman, he compiled a collection of lures as a gift. When Ron presented the lures the man cried. Tallahassee police lieutenant Jo Ann Van Meter got to ride around with her Krasnodar counterparts on police patrol. She reported to our local newspaper that "they make the same stupid jokes, have the same way of doing things, and think the same." There were some differences. She reported that "people taken into custody are not read their rights, and someone can be held for 72 hours without charge." The Russian custom of giving gifts overwhelmed her. "They gave me so many gifts that I was embarrassed."[4] Students studying theater at Florida State University are able to participate in an exchange with the Moscow Art Theater School due to contacts theater school dean Gil Lazier made while visiting Krasnodar. Lazier directed the Russian premier of Neil Simon's "I Oughta Be in Pictures" in Moscow, and six students from our city have already studied at the Moscow Art Theater.

Our sister city program has been a bigger success than any of its originators dreamed. There is now a Tallahassee Street in Krasnodar, and the citizens of Krasnodar are anxious to have our local businesses set up joint enterprises with them. We have had a significant impact on improving relations between our countries. We have witnessed and helped the process of opening up the Soviet Union. When we began, the only direct line to the Soviet Union we had was a computer telecommunications link that sister city activist Bob Broedel set up from Tallahassee. For several years Broedel handled communications for over a dozen sister city programs. Now there are many direct links to the Soviet Union.

Human Rights in the Soviet Union

The Kremlin was impressive, the Pushkin Museum was fantastic, and Moscow is a city whose trees and many waterways were an unexpected pleasure. Still, what does one learn about the Soviet Union by looking at tourist attractions? I wanted to know how free Soviet citizens are, so I visited a Jewish family that wanted to leave the USSR.

Before leaving for the Soviet Union I had contacted the South Florida Conference on Soviet Jewry and been given the names of individuals who had requested to leave the Soviet Union— refuseniks. It is easy to say that the Soviet Union is a totalitarian state and let that be the end of it. Those living in the Soviet Union don't think in terms of absolutes. They remember when things were worse, and they are amazed at the new freedom of expression in the press.

My wife, Judy, and I visited with Ari and Mila Volvovsky at the home of Igor and Irina Gurvich, who were also present along with their children. The apartment had two rooms, besides the kitchen and bathroom. One room served as a dining room, living room, and bedroom for the adults. The children's bedroom was ingeniously set up with a jungle gym. This apartment housed four adults and four children. Because people are not always allowed to get permits to live where they want in the Soviet Union, they have to double up on apartments.

We brought several books and music cassette tapes as gifts. I regret not bringing more books and other items and not having every member of our sister city group bring things. I didn't understand that widely owned items in the United States, like cassette players, cost more than a hundred dollars in Russia—half a month's wages. I didn't understand the thirst for intellectual materials and the need for consumer items.

Ari Volvovsky spent two years in jail for the crime of teaching Hebrew. The Soviet authorities worked on his students, keeping one in the KGB office for ten hours—threatening him with loss of his student deferment and telling him that he would end up in the infantry in Afghanistan—until the student agreed to testify against him. Ari's students were forced to sign lies. The charge was slandering the Soviet state. Ari served part of his sentence in Gorki, the city where he grew up. Although he knows hundreds of people in Gorki, no one had the courage to visit him.

Judy and I felt privileged to be with sincere people like Ari, Mila, Igor, and Irina. Ari is simply trying to do what Jews have done for thousands of years—pass on Jewish traditions. He differs from the early civil rights activists who would not accept second-class citizenship only in his lack of a lawyer. Ari did not appear to have the help of lawyers, and I decided to ask him about this.

I had read that the Soviet Union had changed its laws to allow individuals to have private businesses, provided they do not hire others, so I asked if he had examined the possibility of registering a business to teach Hebrew. Although Ari did not know much about the new laws and did not have much faith in the Soviet legal system, he believed in challenging officials to obey their own laws. He told us that he was not afraid to receive letters from us and that he did things openly. He believed that he was not breaking any laws of the Soviet Union and he wanted the Soviet Union to obey its own laws.

The rights of citizens in the Soviet Union would appear to

depend more on the mood of the leaders than on laws. A totalitarian system was in place but not always enforced. Individuals tried to guess the mood of the leaders. Igor Gurvich thought that his chances of being allowed to emigrate had increased because the government had recently asked him more questions. From the experience of others he thought that a good sign.

Since I have a Macintosh computer and Ari is a computer scientist, we discussed computers. Developments have been so rapid that Ari could not guess how small computers are that can do word processing. I showed him a pamphlet I had typeset on my computer and asked him how large he thought a computer would have to be to do word processing. He guessed the size of a room, then the size of a large table, and was amazed when I told him that I can lift my computer. Ari explained that all computers in the Soviet Union are registered and that no one can own a printing press. Then he showed us how he made copies of instructional materials for his students. He had to photograph materials and develop separate sheets on thick photograph paper.

We asked our hosts what they thought of Gorbachev, glasnost, and peristroika. They told us that they were able to read things they had not been able to read before, especially in the *Moscow News,* but that nothing had really changed. They supported change but didn't think that the Communist bureaucracy would allow real change to occur. They expected Gorbachev to be replaced and just wanted to get out as soon as they could. I later learned that they are now living in Israel. Everywhere we went in the Soviet Union we met people of all ethnic backgrounds who wanted to get out. When we asked a waiter in a restaurant why he wanted dollars instead of rubles, he replied that he wanted to leave the Soviet Union and he needed dollars to do so.

It was obvious to us after seeing how Ari Volvovski made copies of materials for his students that the Soviet Union cannot enter the information age without changing its ways. Whether positive changes will come, time will tell. We felt that we had helped the process.

12

■ ■ ■

American and Soviet Philosophers Discuss Peace

■ ■ ■

Suppose that people from the United States and the Soviet Union were to meet to discuss ways to work for peace. What might they say to each other? I list here some of the issues and viewpoints examined by participants at the International Colloquium On World Peace that met as part of the XVII World Congress of Philosophy in Montreal in August 1983.

The format followed the usual agenda of academic conferences. Each person read a paper on a different topic, and people offered criticisms. (No attempt was made to record when consensus was reached. I would like to see conferences held that centered on a list of agreed-upon issues and recorded areas of agreement and disagreement.) In what follows I attempt, by rearranging the order of papers and commentaries, to line up the participants from the United States and the Soviet Union on issues and to show where participants agreed and disagreed. The issues I have chosen are "Can Modern Warfare Be Just?," "Who Is to Blame for the Arms Race?," "Is Conflict Inevitable due to Differences on Human Rights?," and "What Can Be Done to Ease Tensions?" Because I have done extensive editing, I do not state the names of the participants, although I identify nationalities. Their views are taken out of context without the qualifications contained in their papers.

Can Modern Warfare Be Just?

A retired philosophy professor from the United States argued that we should not use the term "war" to refer to the exchange of nuclear weapons because wars have survivors, and no one could survive a nuclear exchange. He suggested that we use the term "omnicide," coined by Professor John Somerville, to refer to the killing of all. Someone could win a war, but no one could win at omnicide. There is such a thing as a just war or a war of liberation, but there is no such thing as a just omnicide or an omnicide of liberation. One could argue that there is, on occasion, a right, or even a duty, to wage war, and still be considered a sane human being, but if someone were to argue that there is a right or a duty to wage omnicide, he or she would have to be considered insane. We have created the practical possibility of omnicide, and now we must make ourselves face the reality of that possibility in order to prevent ourselves from implementing it in practice.

A philosopher from Poland read a paper on "Nuclear War and Morality: A View From Eastern Europe," in which he analyzed the concept of a just war from both Christian and Marxist perspectives. He examined St. Augustine's claim that a war is just only if it separates combatants from noncombatants so that the innocent are spared. St. Thomas Aquinas built on St. Augustine's views and added that for a war to be just it must be limited in scope and discriminate between combatants and noncombatants. Since there is no way to separate combatants from noncombatants in a nuclear war, and no way to limit such a war, war cannot now be justified according to the Christian perspective.

According to the traditional Marxist perspective, a war is just if it is a war of the oppressed classes for their national liberation. All revolutionary wars are justified and all counterrevolutionary wars are unjustified. From the Marxist perspective, pacifists who speak of war in the abstract instead of from a class perspective should be criticized. The author of this paper, himself a Marxist, then brought the Marxist perspective up to date. He stated his belief that now all has changed because victory is not possible. Today, peace is an independent value. It does not matter which side one favors. Nuclear war cannot be justified because it endangers everyone and thus has no class character—it has a human character. Pacifism is realism today—it is not abstract idealism.

A professor from the United States offered some interesting figures to support the view that nuclear weapons are entirely different from previous weapons. He stated that the Hiroshima and Nagasaki bombs were two to three thousand times more powerful than previously existing bombs of the same weight. This increased their destructive power fantastically. He pointed out that each Trident submarine has a hundred times the destructive capacity of the bombs that fell on Hiroshima and Nagasaki.

Several individuals at the colloquium expressed the view that the planet is threatened with destruction. While agreeing on this, the participants did not agree on who is at fault for the present situation or what to do about it.

Who Is to Blame for the Arms Race?

A philosophy professor from the United States read a paper entitled, "The Arms Race: Genocidal Intent and Responsibility." He argued that, in preparing for nuclear war, both superpowers are committed to genocide. The United Nations defined genocide as the denial of the right of existence to any group, and this definition includes acts intending to destroy racial, ethnic, political, or national groups. According to the canons of international law used at Nuremberg, each of us has a duty to break any bond of complacency in the criminal behavior of our government. Applying this to the present situation he argued that each of us has a duty to oppose preparation for nuclear omnicide.

A professor from the Soviet Union criticized the view that both sides are guilty of genocide in preparing for nuclear omnicide. This speaker claimed that he understood that the deployment of weapons by the Soviet Union was a shock to the United States. He stated that the United States was never vulnerable to attack because it was protected by oceans, and now for the first time the United States is vulnerable. He said that he understood that this is uncomfortable for the United States, but this is a normal situation for a nation. The Soviet Union, Poland, and Hungary are all vulnerable. His conclusion was that the United States would have to learn to live with its vulnerability and not try to achieve domination through weapons.

A political scientist from Canada stated that wars begin in the minds of people and that it is in the minds of people that wars must end. The real enemy is a mind set. Several Soviet philosophers responded. One stated that there are economic causes of war, quoting the Prussian general Karl von Clausewitz: "War is politics by other means." His conclusion was that it is necessary to put cultural factors into context and to see war as the product of economic exploitation due to capitalism. Another argued that by analyzing who benefits from war preparations, it is possible to see clearly that the United States is the culprit in the arms race. The arms manufacturers make money from weapons production and that is why the United States keeps introducing new weapons.

According to one professor from the Soviet Union, the United States has a policy of world domination. "The United States should support United Nations resolutions regarding national liberation movements," he said, and quoted the German philosopher Immanual Kant: "Fulfill your social duty to show what kind of person you are."

A U.S. psychologist read a paper entitled "But What about Our Fear of the Russians?" He stated that the fear of Russia is widespread, and there are some good reasons for some of it. Parts of their ideology and their actions (in Afghanistan and Poland, for example) should concern us. He went on to say that he assumes that the Russians are fearful of us, and with good reasons. Our 1917 invasion of their country in an attempt to end their revolution, and our use of atomic weapons against Japan in 1945 have contributed greatly to their fear of us. His solution was not to dismiss these reciprocal fears but to learn to respond to them more intelligently. There are real differences between us. The conference addressed itself to some of the differences.

Is Conflict Due to Differences on Human Rights?

A U.S. philosophy professor began the discussion with a paper entitled "Are Marxism and Democracy Compatible?" arguing that alternative viewpoints begin with different basic ontologies and that democracies begin with an ontology that places individuals first. Individuals have rights and can form their own associations. In contrast, a Marxist ontology places society ahead of the individual. According to this professor, all individuals have the capacity for freedom, but the right of individuals to be free is not always recognized. Her conclusion was that there is an inevitable conflict between democracy and Marxism because democracy assumes the rights of individuals and Marxism denies these rights.

One immediate response to this professor's talk was an objection by a philosopher from the United States to the terms "democracy" and "human rights." The respondent argued that because everyone today claims that their system is democratic, the word is meaningless and, thus, one cannot speak of democracy versus Marxism. He also criticized the notion that the United States favors human rights and the Soviet Union does not. He argued that each had rights that the other lacked. The rights that the United States stresses are the political rights, such as the right to express unpopular views, while the rights the Soviet Union stresses are economic, such as the right to a job or medical care. He suggested that the rights stressed in the United States be called "blue rights" and those in the Soviet Union be called "red rights." We might add "green rights" to these, which include the right to clean air and water and the rights of living creatures besides humans.

An Indian philosopher said that the Marxist and non-Marxist philosophies are not contradictory, but complementary. If the adherents of each would keep their aims in mind they would see that the aim of communism is economic development and that the aim of the western democracies is political democracy. The two are complementary because one cannot be complete without the other.

A professor from the United States spoke on "The Myth of Ideological Conflict," pointing out historical examples of slogans invented to justify wars started for entirely different reasons. "Wars are touted as being for ideals," he said, "but actually ideology is used more often to rationalize wars that have already started. Conflicts are verbalized and, thus, they seem contradictory and unsolvable. But actually, conflicts are not ideological and can be prevented." He argued for the creation of "the planetary man" by stressing things that all people can relate to, including nature, athletics, art, the natural sciences, and working with the elderly and little children.

All the philosophers present agreed that we sometimes make too much of differences in philosophies. While on paper there are contradictory philosophies, in real life there is broad unexplored area for agreement. We did not resolve the real differences in the area of human rights and democracy, but our discussion indicated areas to explore further.

Part V

Educating for Peace

IN THE LABORATORY OF HUMAN AFFAIRS

Fitzgerald in the *St. Louis Post-Dispatch.*

■ Human history becomes more and more a
race between education and catastrophe.
—H. G. Wells

13

■ ■ ■

Developing Planetary Citizens

■ ■ ■

The abolition of war requires that institutions for settling disputes between nations be strengthened and that people use these institutions. Changing people's consciousness is just as important as changing institutions. Structures for settling disputes are of no use if they are not used.

For international authority structures to succeed in settling disputes, people must act as planetary citizens. Those in the authority structures must act as neutral judges. National leaders must bring their disputes with other nations to the World Court. The citizens of every nation must pressure their national leaders to help establish a new world order. Increasing numbers of people must come to see themselves as planetary citizens. A prerequisite for peace is that people have, in addition to a loyalty to their homeland, a concern for the good of the planet or a planetary consciousness.

The Need for People Everyone Can Trust

Some people fear the replacement of war with a legal system because they don't think that the administrators of a legal system can be fair. Among individuals from particular backgrounds—American, Soviet, German, French—citizens of one country or another, who can we trust to act as neutral administrators? How can we find people that all parties can trust? Is it possible for people to add to their love of their own homeland a planetary consciousness?

Some individuals have developed a planetary consciousness—people who are respected by people throughout the world for being fair and open-minded. We seem to know very little about how to educate people to act as neutral peacemakers. We need a science concerning methods for fostering a planetary consciousness. The study of fairness might begin by examining the methods those in the physical sciences use to counteract the natural impulse to be biased. A scientist learns, for example, to go out of his or her way to include unpleasant hypotheses, because the natural impulse is to omit them. Just as scientists need techniques to force themselves to be open-minded, people interested in becoming planetary citizens need special techniques.

There are groups that are respected by people throughout the world for their objectivity, whose members go out of their way to be objective and to be perceived as such. Amnesty International, a recipient of the Nobel Peace Prize, enjoys an international reputation for fairness. One activist member, Sean MacBride, is the only person to receive the highest awards offered by both the Eastern Bloc countries and the West—the Lenin Peace Prize and the Nobel Peace Prize. How have Amnesty International and those working for it come to enjoy a reputation for objectivity?

Several procedures to insure objectivity within Amnesty International were established by its founder, Peter Benenson, an English citizen who organized it in 1960 after reading a brief newspaper report about two Portuguese students sentenced to seven years in prison for drinking a toast to freedom. He decided to set up an organization that would not allow such prisoners to be forgotten. Each chapter of Amnesty International chooses three prisoners—one from a Communist bloc country, one from the West, and one from the Third World—publicizes their cases, and works for their release. To insure objectivity, no group adopts a prisoner from its own country.

The organization has a well-defined, limited role that people all over the world can understand. Its first goal is to work for prisoners of conscience—people detained for their beliefs, color, sex, ethnic origin, language, or religious creed—with the condition that such persons have not used or advocated violence. Its second goal is to work for prompt trials for all political prisoners. Its third goal is the abolition of the death penalty, torture, and any other cruel, inhuman, or degrading treatment.

From the start, Amnesty International has been effective. One of the first prisoners adopted was Joseph Beran, who, after being imprisoned by the Nazis during the war, became Archbishop of Prague only to be imprisoned by the Czechoslovakian government for giving a sermon. Amnesty International sent letters and telegrams from all over the world, and Sean MacBride visited Czech foreign minister Jiri Hajeck in Prague. After a year-long campaign, Beran was freed. In 1962, a similar campaign of letters, telegrams, and personal visits was conducted on behalf of jailed opponents of Ghana's leader, Kwame Nkrumah. Louis Blom-Cooper visited Ghana on their behalf in 1962 and five months later 152 detainees were released. Prem Kher, a lawyer from India, went to the German Democratic Republic to investigate the case of Heinz Brandt, a trade unionist who was spirited out of West Germany and jailed in East Germany. Kher met with the East German attorney general. His efforts, and an international campaign that included efforts by British philosopher Bertrand Russell, helped secure the release of Brandt within two years.

Amnesty International has 25,000 adoption groups in 140 countries. It is one of the few truly international organizations and that is its main strength. In addition to making the organization more effective in winning the release of prisoners, the adoption of foreign prisoners fosters within members a feeling of being world citizens concerned about their fellow human beings.

Many other groups enjoy a reputation for internationalism. The American Friends Service Committee is welcome everywhere in the world, the Swedish Peace Institute enjoys a reputation for fairness, and the Institute for Strategic Studies and *Jane's Fighting Ships* and other Jane's publications have earned respect worldwide as reliable sources for information on armaments. Part of the study of how to achieve peace is the study of how individuals and groups can learn to be fair and objective.

It is not natural for people to be objective and fair—the normal state is for people to be biased and nationalistic. Nevertheless, just as scientists have worked out methods to combat the natural tendency toward biased research, we can discover ways to help people develop a planetary consciousness.

Communication and Planetary Consciousness

In examining ways to foster a planetary consciousness we might examine activities that increase patriotism. One way to increase a feeling of togetherness is by communicating. Today a world community is possible because today we can have global communications. A common language is one of the main factors that strengthen nationalism. The use of an international language would increase internationalism. People throughout the world feel a special bond to others who speak the same language. Another way is celebrating patriotic holidays: celebrating international holidays would build a planetary consciousness. Perhaps the strongest factor building patriotism is fighting external enemies. Here too, there are lessons for building a planetary consciousness. We can personify and externalize the dangers that threaten human survival and have a campaign to rid ourselves of them.

The world's first communications satellite, launched on April 6, 1965; it weighed only eighty-five pounds and made live, transoceanic, intercontinental television possible. A telephone call from London to New York dropped within a few years from $9.00 to $5.40. It is practical today to communicate with each other. The new communications breakthroughs have made possible one world community. The ideal of Athenian democracy was to have citizens convene in a common place to attend to common business. Aristotle thought that the ideal size of a political unit was determined by the range of a speaker's voice. Today a speaker can be heard anywhere on earth.

Several things are achieved just by the act of communication. We learn how others see us. Instead of Americans guessing what the Soviet reaction may be to an action, communication supplies an answer. The mere fact of communication can force people on both sides to temper what they say about each other. Many American television shows and films display prejudice against Russians, such as when people with Russian accents are portrayed as evil agents in a James Bond film. Russians also defame Americans in their media. Defamations of minorities are reduced in the media when those minorities complain. Where are the Soviet citizens who might complain? If citizens of the United States and the Soviet Union were to communicate directly with each other, these defamations would be reduced.

Perhaps the most significant result of communication would be an inevitable move towards consensus on the issues that divide us. When people communicate in a meaningful way, with argumentation and the presentation of facts, they often convince each other and move toward a common viewpoint. When it is not possible to reach agreement, it is still possible to understand the other person's viewpoint.

Why don't humans use the marvelous communications systems that exist? Some people cite the language barrier, others cite ideological differences. The Association for Humanistic Psychology[1] promotes a simple human exchange that does not involve language or ideology by helping individuals in the United States exchange family photographs with Soviet citizens. People on both sides display these photos to remind themselves that people in other countries are also human. Americans and Russians can communicate directly because many people in the Soviet Union read and write English.[2] Of course, peace is furthered by having all the people of the world communicating, not just citizens of the United States and Soviet Union.[3]

International Language

Because of the tremendous need for an international language, and because no alternative to English has presented itself, English is rapidly becoming the international language. Other languages, such as Esperanto, may be more desirable because they are more neutral, but English is being adopted for international commerce. It is spoken in 44 of 160 countries and uses the same Roman script as Spanish, French, Turkish, Indonesian, and many other languages. Half the scientific literature in the world is now published in English. A writer who wants to be widely read must write in English. The majority of the world's college and university graduates speak English. For better or worse, English is becoming the international language.

There is some resistance to the spread of English because it is a national language. Its spread symbolizes for many cultural and economic domination by the English-speaking powers. The governments of Kenya and India have fought the spread of English by mandating the use of their native languages, Swahili and Hindi, respectively, as the country's official language. The government of Quebec has mandated French as the official language of that province.

Some have proposed Esperanto as the international language because it is culturally neutral and would not encounter the same resentments as English. It would be most desirable if the United Nations would declare one language the favored international language. I favor Esperanto for this role and its potential to promote a planetary consciousness. First of all, learning Esperanto reflects a desire to communicate with people on neutral terrain and marks one as a person who has an international outlook. Second, learning Esperanto draws one closer to others around the world who are ready to embrace internationalism. Part of working for peace is to work to forge a new international identity, and learning Esperanto helps.[4]

International Holidays

Just as national holidays foster patriotism, international holidays foster a planetary consciousness. The United Nations proclaimed October 24 as UN Day, with the recommendation that member states declare it a public holiday. At the same time each year, the end of October, the United Nations International Children and Education Fund, UNICEF, has its annual collection. One way to strengthen planetary consciousness is to celebrate UN Day and work on the UNICEF campaign.

United Nations Day can be celebrated with many small symbolic acts. One can display posters, a United Nations flag, or distribute automobile decals that show Earth photographed from space. Seeing such symbols makes people realize that we are all on one planet. UN Day is an opportunity to increase knowledge of the United Nations and its agencies. The United Nations can claim some accomplishments that we can all be proud of. It has outlived the only previous attempt at forming a global political institution—the League of Nations, which survived for barely twenty years. In the midst of World War II, in 1943, a resolution for a general international peacekeeping organization was adopted by the United States, the Soviet Union, the United Kingdom, and China. Fifty nations signed a charter and the UN was born on October 24, 1945. The number of member nations increased from 50 to 150. The UN now has almost universal membership and is increasingly viewed as a permanent part of international life.

The United Nations has a tremendous impact on the lives of most people on our planet. It supervised the transition of many countries from colonies to independent statehood through its

Trusteeship Council. Many of the struggles against colonialism involved violence, but the United Nations prevented violence in others. Over half the nations in the world were colonies when the United Nations was formed. After becoming independent, nations were able to attain public recognition of their new status as they took their place in the General Assembly. Ninety percent of the UN budget is for aid to the poorer nations in the world.

The United Nations was successful in its response to Iraq's invasion of Kuwait, first by voting to establish sanctions and then by approving the use of force. In the first test of post–cold war cooperation, the world community was able to take united action with twenty-eight nations fighting Iraq to enforce UN resolutions. When we observe the successful outcome of the Persian Gulf War, we should celebrate the new success of the United Nations.

Focusing on a Common Enemy

The most common way of increasing patriotism is to focus on an enemy. Patriotism is strongest in war, especially when there has been an invasion of one's own country. Love for one's own group (amity) is often strengthened by hatred of any enemy (enmity). A direct relationship exists between amity and enmity.

If the nations of the earth were threatened by a common enemy, they would unite to fight that enemy. Indeed, the United Nations was originally the nations united to combat fascism. Today we face common threats in the form of nuclear war and the destruction of the environment. But, unlike the Nazi threat, which people recognized as an external force personified by Hitler, people do not recognize that today's threat can only be met, as the Nazi threat was met, with nations strongly united.

Today we are not meeting the threat as we did when the threat was personal and external. Patriotism was aroused because we could see our enemy and unite against it. To help us see today's threat as an external force I have invented the monster EARTHYUK. EARTHYUK personifies all the threats to life on this planet. To oppose EARTHYUK is to oppose the "yukking up" of our planet. Focusing on an enemy to hate, an enemy that is threatening all life on the planet, can foster a planetary consciousness.

14

■ ■ ■

Peace Studies and Research Centers

■ ■ ■

We know how to kill each other but not how to live together. Over a hundred universities have addressed themselves to this problem by instituting peace studies programs, and new peace research institutes have been established, including the United States Institute of Peace established by Congress. In this chapter I examine these developments. In the next chapter I attempt to demonstrate the usefulness of peace studies by providing short lessons in conflict resolution and game theory.

Educating for Planetary Consciousness

One approach to peace studies, sometimes called global education, involves covering curriculum from many disciplines in a way that fosters a planetary consciousness. The movement to include the accomplishments of non-European cultures in the humanities curriculum has received publicity lately. At many universities, including Stanford, where students demonstrated for the change, humanities courses have been revised to make room for materials on Third World cultures.

Advocates of global education rate curricula according to whether or not they include materials on Third World cultures and nations (Latin America, Asia, and Africa) and whether all viewpoints, including Third World viewpoints, are considered. Are alternative views of the causes of poverty and development considered? Do discussions of human rights include economic rights (for food, shelter, medical care, education, employment, etc.) in addition to civil and political rights? Does ecology include a discussion of ecological limits to economic growth, alternative attitudes we might take to our planet, and how alternative lifestyles affect the planet? A global education aims at providing students with a background to deal with some of the global issues we face, such as the division between rich and poor nations, the conflicts over human rights, and ecological problems.

Why is it important that students learn about the contributions of non-Europeans? Those who know only about European contributions to civilization are more likely to be racists. If one reads the writings of fascist and Nazi theorists, it is apparent that none of them ever learned anything about non-European cultures. One way we help people learn to live together is to encourage them to learn about each other.

Peace studies as a separate discipline includes studying ways to minimize violence and examining alternatives to war and the issue of whether or not war is inevitable. In specific courses, students study methods of conflict resolution and learn about famous peacemakers such as the Reverend Martin Luther King, Jr., and Mohandas K. Gandhi.

Traditional education covers skills that people need in order to live together. By traditional education I mean a background in literature, the arts, and the humanities: the kind of background that people refer to when they say that someone is "well educated." Such traditional standbys as introductory logic courses that teach skills that help people either to agree or to understand why they are disagreeing are essential to those who want to work for peace.

War and the Ability to Perceive Reality

An education for living with others includes knowledge of self, of others, of how others see us, and of how others see themselves. Several wars started because people lacked knowledge in these four areas, among them World War I. When Kaiser Wilhelm II of Germany heard that the Austrian crown prince, Franz Ferdinand, had been assassinated on June 28, 1914, he thought that this act was a threat to all monarchies.[5] If he had known himself better, he would have realized that he was misinterpreting a Serbian patriot's actions because of his own insecurities. The Kaiser then assumed that Czar Nicolas II, also a monarch, would welcome action to punish the "assassins of royalty." The Kaiser sent a letter to the Austrians promising "faithful support" if they took punitive action against Serbia. He did not understand how either the Austrians or the Russians would perceive his actions. The Austrians invaded Serbia. The Czar interpreted this as an action against all Slavic people, rather than an action to protect monarchy. Russia entered the war in defense of Serbia. Because Kaiser Wilhelm had promised to support Austria, not understanding what Austria would do or what the Russian reaction would be, Germany found itself at war with Russia. Each side knew so little about the other that each thought the war would be over in a few weeks.

History is replete with such examples. Before the Korean War, in January 1950, Secretary of State Dean Acheson said in a speech that Korea was outside the U.S. defense perimeter. That statement was interpreted by the North Koreans as an invitation to cross the border with impunity.

Saddam Hussein's invasion of Kuwait may well have been prompted by a misunderstanding of statements made by U.S. officials. On July 24, 1990, nine days before Iraq's invasion of Kuwait and with Iraqi troops massed on Kuwait's border, Secretary of State James Baker's official spokesperson, Margaret Tutwiler, stated, "We do not have any defense treaties with Kuwait, and there are no special defense or security commitments to Kuwait." On July 25 the American ambassador to Iraq, April Glaspie, told Saddam Hussein that "we have no opinion on the Arab-Arab conflicts, like your border disagreement with Kuwait." The last statement is according to minutes of that meeting released by Iraq and not disputed by the United States.[6] These statements might well have given Saddam Hussein reason to think that the United States would not come to the aid of Kuwait. Secretary Baker stated on NBC's "Meet the Press" (Sept. 23, 1990) that the statements by Tutwiler and Glaspie "had to do with taking sides on a border dispute, not taking sides on the question of unprovoked aggression." Had we understood better how Saddam Hussein might understand our statements, and let it be clearly known how we would react to an invasion, Iraq might not have invaded Kuwait.

Many wars might be avoided if we understood better how people in other nations understand our actions. The United States misjudged the chances of winning support in Vietnam. The Vietnamese fought the French for twenty-five years. Whatever the stated goals of the United States in Vietnam, how could anyone think that the Vietnamese would see the United States as anything but another colonial power?

How can people learn to see accurately themselves, others, and how others see themselves? Studying alternative philosophies has been the traditional method. Studying different philosophies, one learns to trace the implications of the alternative premises that people accept. To do this successfully, one must suspend one's own belief system and try to fit into the thinking of others. One also sees how various thinkers have misunderstood each other. This is one of the most challenging and rewarding experiences a person can have and guarantees growth in one's ability to understand other people.

Peace Studies Programs

There are over two hundred peace studies programs in U.S. universities, most of which were started during the 1970s. Several good guides to these programs exist. *Peace and World Order Studies: A Curriculum Guide* provides actual course syllabi under such headings as alternative world order, international organization and law, economic development and well being, human rights, and ecological balance.[7] *The Guide to Careers and Graduate Education in Peace Studies* claims that graduate programs fall roughly into six areas: peace and justice in the religious context; general peace and conflict studies; conflict resolution; citizen participation in socio-economic development; arms control and international security; and public interest law and/or alternative dispute resolution.[8]

The authors of the *Guide to Careers* and many other writers on peace education, such as Betty A. Reardon, differentiate between negative peace and positive peace in their descriptions of peace education. According to Reardon, "Most recent teaching has focused on negative peace—that is, on reducing the likelihood of war. It has emphasized the problems posed by arms races and specific cases of international conflict, and it falls within what I classify as the reform approach to peace education. However, although the wider emphasis is on negative peace and the focus is on the problem of armed conflict, the subject of study is not so much *war* as *wars*. Most current peace education does not address war as an institution." She goes on, "Positive peace has become the concept connoting a world in which the need for violence has been significantly reduced; if not eliminated. The major areas of concern in the domain of positive peace are the problems of economic deprivation and development; environment and resources; and universal human rights and social justice. Peace education seems to have subsumed all these areas into the general concept of global justice."[9]

Every person involved in peace studies cannot be thoroughly informed on all aspects of the subject. Political science departments tend to have courses or programs related to international studies, the United Nations, and other international institutions. Colleges of education tend to have programs in international education and intercultural studies. Philosophy, religion, history, economics, psychology, anthropology, English, and sociology departments all have their own particular emphasis. Where a peace studies program is placed in an educational curriculum depends on the individuals interested in the program and the internal workings of the university. Courses tend to reflect the academic discipline of the individuals and groups involved.

As programs were initiated in the seventies, interest grew in making peace studies a distinctive field. This interest assumed that peace encompassed a clearly defined area of knowledge—an assumption rejected by many today. While the boundaries of peace studies cannot be clearly delineated, some areas definitely fall within its purview, such as conflict resolution. (One can demonstrate that peace studies can make a unique contribution by showing the benefits of studying conflict resolution, which I will do in the next chapter.)

Peace education has found a place in the elementary and secondary school curriculum. Some excellent materials on how to handle conflict have been developed for elementary school children.[10] Instruction in conflict resolution can make a difference in areas where children might otherwise be overwhelmed by gangs and violence. While the skills taught in peace studies are important on a global level, they are also important in our personal relationships.

Peace Research Centers

The real test of peace studies is whether scholars in this field make actual contributions to peace. Peace research centers have already made tremendous contributions to peace, among them the International Peace Academy,[11] which helped in the historic Camp David Accords that ended the state of war between Egypt and Israel.

Action oriented, the International Peace Academy has programs for practitioners in international relations and also aids universities. It tries to be relevant and useful by producing papers that are useful to people involved in current international conflicts.

In the Camp David discussions, both Egypt and Israel sent participants to the academy and, at their request, the academy made up a simulation that helped Israelis and Egyptians discuss the disengagement of troops in the Sinai. The simulation, based on facts readily available from newspaper reports, required both sides to play through the steps of reaching an agreement. Israeli and Egyptian negotiators who took part in the academy's simulations learned how to reach the actual agreement on the withdrawal of Israeli troops. The plans worked out in the simulation, which involved having UN troops move in to provide a buffer, were actually used.

The United States Institute of Peace was created in 1984 with a mandate to expand knowledge about the nature of war and peace, to provide lessons from that knowledge in a form that can be used by decision makers, and to help educate the American public on ways to increase the chances for peace.[12] The institute was set up to be analogous to the National Endowment for the Humanities and the National Science Foundation and to operate like a public foundation. Funded grants already include "new approaches to conflict management" in addition to traditional research and scholarship.

One institute that amateur scholars can participate in is the Peace Research Institute.[13] In addition to other work, it publishes more than 500 abstracts of peace-related publications a month in the *Peace Research Abstracts Journal.* The work of abstracting, done by volunteers from around the world, is interesting and important.

One final organization is an umbrella group that provides information on all peace research and education organizations. Founded in 1970, the Consortium on Peace Research, Education, and Development (COPRED) publishes *Peace Chronicle* and *Peace and Change,* in which it reviews publications, provides information on peace studies programs, and informs readers about grants and conferences related to peace.[14]

15

▪ ▪ ▪

Lessons in Conflict
Resolution and
Game Theory

▪ ▪ ▪

People have always been interested in learning ways of resolving conflicts. Even people who want to wage war prefer to have those on their own side resolve their conflicts without violence. It is only recently, however, that a scientific approach to conflict resolution has attempted to observe what works in negotiations and mediation.

In what follows I first present concepts of conflict resolution that might be covered in a course in conflict resolution. Studying ways to help mediators be more effective is one function of the new science of conflict resolution. Another is to study the structure of conflict, to try to devise a model that can show the interests of each party in a conflict situation. I introduce some methods of game theory after presenting the basic concepts of conflict resolution.

Basic Concepts of Conflict Resolution

In analyzing conflict it is useful to separate interests from issues. Interests are end results that will satisfy people's needs. Issues or positions are views people hold regarding how to get what they need. People may differ on issues or positions while agreeing on interests. A conflict is a real or perceived state of competing interests.

One can respond in various ways to the existence of conflict. One way is to avoid facing the fact that one's interests compete with other people's interests. This is called conflict avoidance. Another approach is capitulation, which occurs when one party in a conflict decides to forego his or her interests in favor of the other. In discussing conflict resolution we are not discussing conflict avoidance or capitulation. We are discussing approaches that recognize the existence of conflict and the desire of both parties to get the best deal they can.

Conflict resolution includes the various methods that might be used to help people come to agreements that will satisfy the parties—at least to the point that the agreements will be kept. *Conciliation* is the process of helping to get the parties together and talking. A *conciliator* is not involved in the resolution of the conflict and does not have to play a neutral role. When two parties try to resolve a conflict on their own they are *negotiating.* Each party aims at satisfying its basic self-interest, but they must moderate this so that promises made will be kept. *Arbitration* and *mediation* involve an active third party in dispute settlement, the other parties being those who are in conflict. An *arbiter* has the authority to make the decision which is usually final and binding. The arbiter plays a neutral role and judges each case on its merits. In contrast to an arbiter, a mediator has no power. A *mediator* helps the parties decide their own process and decision settlement. A skillful mediator helps the parties develop options and uses caucusing to help them see options realistically so that they can come to an agreement that all can accept.

Mediation is the role that individuals working for peace are most likely to play. Mediation is used in courtroom situations when a judge asks disputants to try to reach an agreement and assigns a mediator to help them. Mediation also occurs when counselors try to help families resolve conflicts and when individuals act as international peacemakers. People can learn to be successful mediators. There is a body of knowledge describing what works and what does not work in mediation, identifiable skills that successful mediators have and that unsuccessful mediators lack, and procedures that can increase the chances of success in mediation.

A successful mediator tries to understand the entire situation, which involves using questioning skills to discover the facts and requires creativity to help participants find a possible settlement range. While the settlement is the participants', the mediator helps them think of new possibilities, test the reality of possible settlements, and, of greatest importance, bring the discussion to closure with a settlement that all can accept.

A skillful mediator understands that some strategies are more likely than others to result in settlements. *Competition* is a strategy one party may follow that would, if successful, result in that party getting all of what it wants, while the other party gets nothing. *Compromise* is a strategy that aims at give-and-take so that each party gets half of what it wants. *Collaboration* is a strategy that involves the integration of interests so that each party helps the other get what it wants while still protecting its own interests. Settlements that involve collaboration are more likely to be accepted because everyone can win following this approach, whereas competition has a winner and a loser and compromise gives the parties only half of what they want.

The easiest way to understand the role of mediators is to do simulations of conflict situations, with people playing the parts of the parties to a conflict and the part of a mediator bringing the parties together.[15]

Those who have had experience in mediation, or those who have done mediation games, know that some things work better than others. For example, focusing on interests works better than focusing on positions. An example that illustrates this distinction is provided by Roger Fisher and William Ury of the Harvard Negotiation Project.

> Consider the story of two men quarreling in a library. One wants the window open and the other wants it closed. They bicker back and forth about how much to leave it open: a crack, halfway, three quarters of the way. No solution satisfies them both.
> Enter the librarian. She asks one why he wants the window open: "To get some fresh air." She asks the other why he wants it closed: "To avoid the draft." After thinking a minute, she opens wide a window in the next room, bringing in fresh air without a draft.[16]

In this example, positions are represented by the position of the window and interests are what each person needs. Each party thought he could satisfy his needs (fresh air or no draft) by having the window in a different position. But often many different means of achieving the same end exist, so focusing on the interests (or ends) works better than focusing on the positions (or means) that people think will achieve their ends.

The example also illustrates that seeking mutual gain or collaboration works better than seeking compromise. A compromise would have been to have the window half open. Neither party would have been satisfied. It is better to try to provide one party with fresh air and to have the other avoid the draft because that way they will both be satisfied.

Another lesson conflict resolution practitioners and theorists have learned is that reaching an agreement is easier when objective criteria are used. When settlements are not based on objective criteria, people pit their wills against each other. The fault with this is that one party wins and the other loses, and no one wants to lose.

There can be more than one objective standard. Consider this example. A house has burnt down and the owner has a dispute with the insurance company over the price. Both parties might agree that a fair standard of value is the replacement cost, the market value, or what a court would most likely award. If the criterion is an objective standard then it is one that the insurance adjuster and the home owner would accept even if each were in the other's position.

Objective criteria also include the use of fair procedures. If a procedure is fair, then either party in the dispute would be willing to take the other party's position. An example of this is the tried and proven method of dividing a piece of cake. One cuts and the other chooses. Which person does the cutting and which does the choosing doesn't matter much.

Some real-life examples will illustrate these principles of conflict resolution. Objective criteria were used to overcome an impasse during the Law of the Sea Conference.[17] India, representing the Third World bloc, proposed an initial fee for companies mining in the deep seabed of $60 million per site. The United States wanted no fee, and a battle of wills ensued. Then both sides agreed to use a model for the economics of deep-seabed mining that had been worked out at the Massachusetts Institute of Technology. That model showed that the proposed $60 million fee would make it impossible for a company to mine, but that some initial fee was economically feasible. As a result both the United States and India changed their positions.

The Camp David Accords illustrate the difference between compromise and collaboration. Before the accords, Israel held the Sinai Desert, which it had taken from Egypt. In simulations I have done, students acting the parts of Egypt and Israel who attempt to compromise by dividing the Sinai do not reach agreement, while students seeking collaboration come up with an agreement identical to the actual settlement. That settlement is a good example of collaboration because Egypt got all of the Sinai and Israel got limits on the placement of tanks near its border; thus, Egypt had all its land returned and Israel received all the security guarantees it needed.

Game Theory

Some progress has been made in the attempt to use mathematical models for understanding the behavior of people in conflict situations, game theory. A pioneer in this field, John von Neumann, combined his interest in poker and his interest in mathematics to produce, along with Oskar Morgenstern, a new mathematical approach to reflect the dependence of each person's winnings and losses on the moves of others in the game.[18] In order to examine the best strategy for any player, you must figure the best strategy for each other player.

A famous example, "The Prisoner's Dilemma," illustrates how to show the outcomes for two players. You and another person have committed a crime, only the police have no evidence against you for that crime. They do have evidence against you on a lesser crime and tell you that if you turn your partner in before your partner turns you in they will dismiss all charges against you and charge your partner with both crimes. They offer the same deal to your partner. If both talk at the same time both are charged with the lesser crime, and if neither talks you are still a suspect in both crimes. The police cleverly interview you and your partner separately, so you have no way of telling whether your partner has tattled on you. Your problem is to decide whether to act cooperatively with your partner, or to act aggressively and turn your partner in.

In this model, cooperative behavior is represented by not talking and aggressive behavior is represented by turning the other person in before they get you. Because the example is one of prisoners who have committed crimes, the example may seem confusing. Fortunately, other models offer the same lessons.

Imagine two primitive food-gatherers: one picks berries and

the other grows vegetables. They would be better off if they shared their food, but one would win big, at least in the short term, if he or she takes without giving in return. We can quantify the results of each action to show its relative value. The assignment of the actual values is arbitrary. If no one steals and they trade berries for vegetables, both get +1. If one robs and is not robbed the one doing the robbing gets +10 and the other gets –10. Each gets –1 if they rob each other.

Both dilemmas illustrate the choice we have of whether to try to dominate or learn to live with others. When all players cooperate the result is better for all than when all players are aggressive. However, when one player is aggressive and the other is cooperative the aggressive one comes out ahead. One might think that both players are better off if they are cooperative. This is not the case. When one is cooperative and the other is aggressive, the aggressive one has the advantage.

Which is the better strategy? Our result is very odd indeed. What is rational to do when considering the actions of both and assuming that both will do the same thing is not the same as what is rational for each to do when the parties consider only themselves. If both consider only themselves, the rational choice is to be aggressive, since the outcome for robbing another (+10) is greater than the outcome when no one robs (+1). But if this is rational for one, then it is also rational for the other, with the net result that all players are hooked into being aggressive, which as we saw before is not as desirable as their both being cooperative (–1 for each as opposed to +1).

Alan Newcombe of the Dundas Peace Research Center has used models patterned after the prisoner's dilemma in doing research.[19] He first recorded the normal response—the response before varying factors—and found that 75 percent of the time, players settle on being cooperative. Then he had one player act aggressively all the time, another act cooperatively all the time, another mirror the moves the others made, and another try cooperative initiatives while responding to aggression with aggression. The purpose was to discover the strategy that would best encourage cooperative behavior.

Newcombe discovered that when one player acted aggressively all the time, the cooperative moves of the other player dropped from the 75 percent normal response to only 6 percent, because a person who wants to cooperate gives up and starts to choose aggressive behavior. When players are always cooperative no matter what other players do, they encourage aggressive behavior on the part of others, because the other players can exploit a cooperative player by being aggressive. Thus, if players act either aggressively all the time or cooperatively all the time, they encourage aggressive behavior. When a player chooses a tit-for-tat strategy, which consists of responding in kind to whatever other players do, cooperative behavior rises to 85 percent. The queen strategy goes beyond tit-for-tat by occasionally introducing cooperative behavior, while still reciprocating aggressive moves. This strategy can increase the level of cooperation to over 90 percent. It works by showing the other players that cooperative behavior is desired even by those who respond to aggression with aggression.

Practical Uses of Peace Research

Work with game theory shows that cooperative behavior can be increased if one side takes the initiative by acting cooperatively and provides an opportunity for the other side to reciprocate. This strategy is the basis of the Graduated Reciprocation in Tension-Reduction, psychologist Charles Osgood's GRIT proposal.[20] Following the GRIT proposal for reducing tension, one party makes a series of conciliatory moves, announcing each in advance and inviting the other party publicly to reciprocate.

President Kennedy made a series of unilateral conciliatory moves in 1963 that culminated in the treaty that banned nuclear testing in the atmosphere. The moves included unilaterally stopping nuclear tests in the atmosphere and approving sales of wheat to the Soviet Union. One researcher who studied the steps, Amatai Etzioni, noted, "For each move that was made, the Soviets reciprocated. . . . They participated in a 'you move–I move' sequence rather than waiting for simultaneous, negotiated, agreed upon moves. Further, they shifted to multilateral-simultaneous arrangements once the appropriate mood was generated.[21] Leaders need to draw on the work of peace researchers to make sure they do not miss opportunities to reduce tension.

Peace research can answer many age-old questions regarding peace. Is it better to turn the other cheek or is it always better to act aggressively when faced with an aggressor? Work with game theory shows that it is best to initiate conciliatory behavior, but to respond in kind to aggression.

Peace research consists of much more than conflict resolution and game theory. Much of this research involves looking for correlations between various factors and the incidence of war. A comparison of national expenditures on defense from 1950 to 1978 shows that increased spending is correlated with an increased likelihood of war,[22] which suggests that the saying of Vegetius, *Si vis pacem, para bellum* (if you want peace, prepare for war) is false. The truth is *Si bellum paras, fiet bellum* (if you prepare for war, war is produced), and the most accurate maxim is *Si vis pacem, para pacem* (if you want peace, prepare for peace). Peace researchers are showing us how to prepare for peace.

Part VI

Thinking Globally, Acting Locally

Reprinted with permission of King Features Syndicate, Inc.

■ *Ideas won't keep.* Something has to be done about them.

—Alfred North Whitehead

16

■ ■ ■

Doing Your Share
for Peace

■ ■ ■

Individuals concerned about peace have to decide whether to translate their concern into action, and if they are committed to doing something they must decide how much time to spend, where to spend that time, and what policies to advocate. In this chapter I begin with a discussion of whether or not it is worth working for peace and then consider what might be accomplished with different amounts of time. In the next three chapters I contrast working in communities with working on the national level, outline brainstorming techniques for thinking of things to do, and show how the theoretical framework developed in this book can serve as a guide to choosing policies to support.

Why Work for Peace?

Many people believe that it is inevitable that we will annihilate ourselves. Advances in technology have made possible atomic, biological, and chemical warfare capable of destroying all life. If current trends continue, we are headed for annihilation. Some people who see these trends try to make changes; others who see them believe working for change is a waste of time and either try to forget the problems or give in to feelings of despair. The problem discussed here is whether extinction is inevitable or whether it is worthwhile working to change the present trend toward extinction.

People say that extinction is inevitable because they see factors that, left alone, will bring it about. They are right. Atomic, biological, and chemical warfare could each by itself bring about human extinction—not to mention the ecological crisis, population explosion, and other problems. However, the claim that extinction is inevitable contains a paradox. People wouldn't say that extinction is inevitable if they didn't see factors that could bring about extinction; yet in seeing these factors people see how to avoid extinction—by removing the factors.

What would it mean to say that extinction is inevitable in the sense of there being nothing that could possibly be done to change the situation? Things would be hopeless if people were dying from unknown causes. We know our afflictions. It is because we see the dangers to life that we fear extinction. Instead of being paralyzed because we see conditions sufficient for bringing about our extinction, we can examine those conditions to see what we have to do to insure survival. We can turn the question around and ask "What is necessary for survival?"

Finding the conditions necessary for survival won't prove that we can succeed in avoiding extinction. The claim that we can avoid extinction rests on two assumptions. First, factors exist which, if changed, would allow us to avoid annihilation, and second, we will be able to make the necessary changes. So far we have provided an answer to condition one. Can we succeed in making the necessary changes? We can't know. Our beliefs regarding the future require an act of faith. While we can't verify statements about the future, it sometimes makes sense to take stands on questions we cannot verify. We all believe things we cannot prove. Of the following pairs of contradictory statements, consider whether we can prove that one is true and the other false.

> Humans have a future.   Humans have no future.
> I can improve the world.   I cannot improve the world.
> I will not die tomorrow.   I will die tomorrow.

My response to the claim that it is not worthwhile to try to make changes because annihilation is inevitable is that we have to make assumptions about the future in order to live our lives. Most of us live as though we will be living tomorrow, yet none of us can be sure. People working for change live as though they will be able to succeed, while they could be wasting their time. Each person has to decide whether to make the effort, and the possibility of change isn't the main factor in this decision. The question is whether it is healthier to struggle than to despair. I choose to struggle.

Consider the following conversation between an active person and an apathetic individual and think of how it might continue.

> Active: "People are in great danger, we must do something."
> Apathetic: "You would need a lot of people to be successful."
> Active: "Yes, that's why you should join me."
> Apathetic: "But you and I aren't enough."
> Active: "I know. We need a lot of people."
> Apathetic: "If you don't have a lot of people our efforts will be wasted. If you have a lot of people then you won't need me. So either my efforts will be wasted or you won't need me."

The puzzle in the last response results from viewing an individual in isolation from other people. I believe that we are responsible for acting as we would want other aware people to act. I would want people who are aware of the dangers that humanity faces to work to remove those dangers, and I do not expect others to do my share.

Why should you work for peace? Isn't it the fault of the people in the military-industrial complex that we have war? You're not the cause, so why should you have to be part of the cure?

Before we can hold a person responsible for a condition such as war, certain things must hold. People are only sometimes responsible for their actions. When people don't know the consequences of their actions, or don't see that they had a choice of actions, it is hard to blame them for consequences. Many people don't believe that peace is a possibility. The most responsible people are those who realize that we can abolish war by instituting a system of enforceable international law. Those who have the vision of a world without war have the greatest responsibility to work for peace.

Working Full-Time

Sometimes people become so concerned about the need to work for peace that they drop everything they are doing and spend all their time at it. This is how a Caravan for Human Survival was initiated in 1982 by Don Gilbert, a sixty-four-year-old surveyor with the municipal water department in Miami. Don had no organization behind him when he started his caravan. He was not an experienced speaker, and he had never even been in the peace movement. The Iranian hostage crisis was the stimulus that stirred him to action.

He read about the Americans being taken hostage just as you and I read of it, and he feared that this crisis or another one might lead to a nuclear holocaust. Don told me that he thought, "I'm scared, but what can I do? I'm not a leader. I'm not an organizer. I'm a nobody."

Don Gilbert isn't a nobody, and neither are we. Instead of asking "What can *I* do?" with the emphasis on the word *"I,"* he told me when I interviewed him in Miami, he asked the question with the emphasis on the word "can," "What *can* I do?" Asked the first way, the person is assuming that he or she is a nobody, incapable of doing anything. Asked the second way, the person is seriously wondering what he or she might do. Don asked the question the second way, and that made all the difference.

One thing that Don did was attend a peace rally at Miami's Torch of Friendship Park. Sixty-four at the time, he and his twenty-two-year-old son Billy carried signs that read World Law or World War. After the rally—Don's first—he and Billy thought of carrying their signs from Miami to Washington. Then they thought that it might be more effective if they stopped at campuses along the way. Because Don believes that the way to peace is through world law, he thought he would contact the largest group advocating this approach, the World Federalist Association.

When Don appeared before a meeting of the association asking for help for his Caravan for Human Survival, his message was, "I'm doing a caravan, and it will be more effective with your help." As he put it, he didn't say, "May I?" or "Can I?" or "If you help me, then I'll do a caravan." He said, "I'm doing it, and I'd like you to join me." He explained, "If you're going to wait for a committee, then you're not going to get anything done." He thought that it might end up with just him and his son Billy going to Washington. Don had already decided to leave his job to work full-time on the caravan.

Don Gilbert told me that the motivating factor behind his commitment to the caravan was the feeling that he owed something to three close friends who had died in World War II while Don had been spared. As a survivor, Don felt that he owed it to his friends to try to insure that no one ever died in wars again.

I met Don Gilbert when the caravan arrived in my hometown, Tallahassee, after it had visited Tampa and Pensacola. I couldn't tell it from the speech I heard, but Don was still very nervous about speaking in public. At this third stop in the caravan, Don had found it necessary to take tranquilizers before each speech. His talk in favor of world law was coherent, and I think quite convincing. While I had been active in the peace movement years earlier and thought that the abolition of war required its replacement with world law, I had not been active recently and had not joined any organization that advocated world peace through world law. As a result of meeting Don Gilbert, I became active again and joined the World Federalist Association.

In his individualistic way, Don Gilbert says that he neither recommends that others do what he did nor recommends against such action. He feels that the crowds were too small and the entire project was much too expensive. Instead of the thousands of marchers he expected in Washington, there were only a few hundred. Don Gilbert had expected to spend about $5,000 on the Caravan for Human Survival and ended up spending $25,000, an enormous amount for a working man.

I include the story about Don Gilbert's caravan because he inspired me. He shows what an individual can do, and his story shows that we need to exercise control in terms of time, money, and effort. We can all do something, but we need not try to do it all ourselves.

Working an Hour a Week

If a few million individuals would work an hour a week for peace and direct their efforts intelligently, it would be possible to abolish war. To be an active member of a peace group, a person might attend one meeting a month and be on one committee—activities that should require no more than about four hours a month. Too often in volunteer organizations, a small core of people overburden themselves, complain that no one else is doing anything, and then burn out. The result is that people become afraid to volunteer to work for peace or anything else. I will show you that you can work for peace without disrupting your life and that it can be pleasant for you to do so.

People fear being overwhelmed by involvement in organizations. We all like to exercise some control over our time. I quit being active in one organization because I found myself being the guest speaker, publicity person, and vice president—all because other people were not doing their jobs. I quit another because one individual kept assigning me to tasks without checking with me. I like being in an organization that lists tasks and tries to get new people involved, instead of overburdening its members.

The secret of having an organization grow is to have exciting projects, divide tasks so that there are lots of little things to do, and invite people to help. In the case of a benefit concert, a dozen tasks can involve twenty people. Publicity involves contacting the newspapers, designing and putting up posters, designing and producing programs, preparing tickets, selling tickets, taking tickets, ushering at the performance, and doing all the tasks connected with the performance itself. None of these tasks by itself is overwhelming. Things get overwhelming when individuals try to do everything by themselves. That is not good for them and it is not good for the organization.

Working Fifteen Minutes a Month

One way to work for peace is to be part of a network of people who write to elected officials expressing their views on global issues. There are three types of alert networks: national mail-alert, national phone-alert, and local phone-alert, and each has its advantages and limitations.

A national mail-alert provides direct communication between those monitoring Congress and concerned citizens who write letters. A brief mail-alert is sent to each network member when a pertinent bill is pending in Congress, typically eight times a year. The alert explains the bill and attempts to motivate the network member to write his or her congressperson. The main advantages to this network are the ease of recruiting a large number of members and alerting them automatically by mail with minimal organizational effort.

Currently the largest national mail-alert network is the Nuclear Arms Alert Network of Common Cause, an organization with 250,000 members.[1] This group supports a bilateral nuclear-weapons freeze. Another group that monitors Congress is the combined SANE-FREEZE, which has about 175,000 members.[2] Neither network requires fees or membership in the organization to be a network member.

Sending letters to members of Congress is an effective way to influence legislation. To strongly and effectively pressure an uncommitted member of the House of Representatives, the representative should receive no fewer than a thousand letters and calls, a week or two before the vote. Letters have a greater impact than calls.

It is very difficult, probably impossible, to influence significantly representatives who consistently vote against your cause. Do not waste your efforts on them. Concentrate only on persons you are likely to influence, "swing" congresspersons. You can recognize them by their mixed voting patterns, both for and against nuclear-weapons-related bills. Voting records on nuclear arms issues can be obtained by writing to the Friends Committee on National Legislation.[3]

To generate one thousand letters and calls, two thousand people per congressional district need to be alerted by various local and national networks, because usually half of the people write. Because a large percentage of people do not like to write often, it is important to ask them to write only when important congressional votes are pending.

Most people do not write to their representatives, so those who do write have a disproportionate influence. Being part of a network is a highly effective way to work for peace without spending much time. It only takes fifteen minutes a month to write one or two short letters. The network sends all the relevant information, so it is not necessary, although of course desirable, for a network member to read large amounts of material. Belonging to the network does not cost anything and people are contacted less than once a month.

Both national and local phone alerts can be effective. A national phone-alert network can provide a quick response to changing congressional developments and, due to the personal nature of the contact, it is more effective in motivating people to act. Local phone-alert networks are usually set up by local peace groups or chapters of national organizations. The local networks are usually smaller than the organization's full local membership, because only a fraction of the membership is willing to be actively involved. Several small networks (under fifty members) are more likely to operate effectively than one large unit. One common problem is having some portion of the network break down during alerts. Systematic checks are required to minimize these breakdowns. Phone networks continually lose callers because people either burn out or the networks are infrequently used. Phone networks require capable and active leadership to maintain them in effective order, which is difficult to accomplish, especially on a long-term basis.

There are thousands of ways that people can work for peace that are pleasant and do not require much time. You should not feel that working for peace is an all or nothing proposition. What is really needed is people who will systematically spend small amounts of time.

17

■ ■ ■

Working for Peace
in Your Community

■ ■ ■

The actual work for peace has to be done by people in local communities who volunteer to do specific tasks. I have been active in a peace group in Tallahassee—the Tallahassee Peace Coalition. Using this organization as a model, I will share the importance of community peace centers, the problems that centers face, how to finance a center, and the things peace center volunteers do. In appendix A, I list activities an individual working in a community peace center might engage in.

Importance of Community Peace Centers

Active peace groups in local communities are the foundation of a healthy movement. A national peace organization that has no local connections has leaders who speak only for themselves. We need active local groups if the peace movement is to mobilize actions and votes throughout the United States.

Community peace organizations provide a way for individuals concerned about peace to become active. Concern alone is not enough. For concern to translate into action, individuals must meet with other concerned people and find things that they can do. The function of a peace group is to increase people's concern, to provide for person-to-person communications so that people can share their concerns, and to provide people with specific things that they can do to help the situations that concern them.

The Tallahassee Peace Coalition is a broadly based coalition of people of differing backgrounds who share a concern about peace. Members of many different organizations and philosophies are part of the coalition—from advocates of enforceable world law, like myself, to people who believe that physical coercion should never be used. All are free to publicize the causes they champion and to gather members for related organizations.

The coalition has several ongoing activities and committees that spearhead them. A political action committee researches bills before Congress, and, through a Legislative Alert, informs the membership by telephone when communication with elected officials would be useful. A membership outreach committee communicates with members to match individuals' interests to committees, such as the newsletter, fundraising, community outreach, and political action.

It is important that people who express an interest in working for peace accept responsibility for particular tasks. A list of the committees in the Tallahassee Peace Coalition and the specific tasks of each is provided in appendix B. If you want to work with a community peace organization or to start one this list may be helpful to you. You might look over the list and choose something that interests you. Pick something that you would enjoy doing and that will give you a sense of accomplishment.

Problems Facing Local Groups

The Tallahassee Peace Coalition has faced the same problems as other local groups and has come up with some solutions. One problem is that many more people express an interest in doing something for peace than end up working with the coalition. In our city of 100,000 we collected 15,000 signatures for a nuclear freeze, yet only a few hundred people subscribe to our newsletter, and usually only about twenty people attend our meetings. To close this gap in membership involvement it is necessary to contact people personally and match people to tasks that interest them.

Another problem of local peace groups, and, indeed, of anyone who wants to work for peace, is finding ways to avoid feeling overwhelmed. Trying to do everything at once soon causes burnout. The solution is dividing the work into discrete tasks that can be accomplished. To further a feeling of accomplishment, committees can list their goals and monitor their progress toward them. When milestones are reached, people rightfully feel that they are being effective in working toward peace.

A third problem is that many national organizations inundate local groups with calls for national campaigns, expecting the local groups to drop whatever they are doing to respond to a national call. National groups spend more time guarding their turf in relation to other national groups than they do in helping local groups develop, although the important work for peace has to be done on the local level. If a peace movement is to become a major force, more people must be reached, and they can best be reached in the communities where they live.

A fourth problem is that many people want to do something for peace but do not have the time. The solution we have found is to hire individuals to work for our peace coalition. There is, of course, plenty of work to do. The problem is money for salaries.

Financing a Community Peace Center

Perhaps the biggest problem facing a community peace center is raising money for ongoing maintenance. There are people with money who would like to do something for peace. To get them to donate, you must convince them that you have an effective organization, that you will use their money to accomplish something. This effort is more successful if you have clear plans about reaching goals so that you can tell potential donors how their money will be used and what will be accomplished.

Local groups have to compete for financial aid with national groups, who have advantages in that they can do mass mailings and have expertise in raising funds. More than a hundred national peace groups send out appeals for funds. It would be helpful if national organizations helped local groups set up mass mailing campaigns for funds and provided traveling consultants to run workshops on planning, publicity, and other topics.

Planning for Success

Anyone can do a mediocre job. However, success requires planning. Groups can be more effective by working out plans for increasing membership, increasing the number of volunteers, and aiming their efforts intelligently.

There has been a movement during the past few years toward using marketing techniques for nonprofit organizations. Although some people dislike the idea of applying marketing concepts, the issue is not one whether to use marketing techniques or not. Any group has to market itself to its volunteers and its ideas to the public it is trying to convince. The issue is the degree of success. Using the marketing model, we might ask who the client is that a peace organization serves. The client is the volunteer who wants to make a contribution to peace. An organization that provides satisfactory experiences to its volunteers will grow and one that doesn't will stagnate. How a group conducts its meetings and how it treats its members determines whether it will grow.

At a business meeting people should list everything that has to be done and divide up the tasks. So that people feel free to suggest tasks, the moderator of a meeting should not automatically assign a task to the person who suggests it. If every time you suggest an action you are stuck with another thing to do, you will stop opening your mouth. The proper time for assigning tasks is after all the tasks are listed, so that people can easily see what their fair share of the work will be.

Good organizers try to match volunteers' needs to those of the organization, and they focus on the needs of the volunteers. They go out of their way to make volunteers feel that they are succeeding in their desire to do something useful. People who join a peace group want to do something for peace, but they don't want tasks dumped on them. They aren't giving anyone a license to boss them around, and they don't want anyone to make them feel guilty for not doing more. Like any healthy person, they want to feel good doing something good. A properly run peace group provides a service to its members.

What does a plan consist of? It might include researching your group's image in the community, then comparing that image with what you think it should be and outlining steps to change it. Planning also involves setting long-range goals for the organization and filling in the steps to reach those goals.

Various types of activities will appeal to different groups of people. Chapters of the World Federalist Association working for world peace through world law can involve lawyers in their activities. Sister city programs for exchanges between American and Soviet cities can involve people in both the arts and athletics. A political action for peace group can involve political activists. Peace research centers can involve local academics, and action against military interventions can be led by university students. These groups do not compete because they involve different segments of the population. A local peace coalition might be most effective by starting several groups and then coordinating and publicizing activities.

Three questions should help any peace organization to examine what it is doing. First, does the movement want to grow and encompass a broad section of the population of the city or confine itself to a small segment of the population? Second, does it want to propose solutions that a majority can potentially embrace or advocate views that limit the size of the group? Third, is it getting together primarily to make members feel better, or is its main interest making a contribution to peace?

How a group answers these questions will determine who speaks for it, which activities it chooses, and whether it does a serious analysis of alternative strategies. The choices are not mutually exclusive. Being involved in a peace movement can make you feel better as you do effective work for peace.

18

■■■

Brainstorming Ways to Work for Peace

■■■

Nobody knows everything about how to work for peace. It is useful to have some general goals and to get together with other people to think of specific things to do. A good way to do it is with a brainstorming session. In this chapter I outline how brainstorming sessions on ways to work for peace might be conducted and share the results of a brainstorming session on positive steps for peace (appendix B).

Brainstorming Techniques

The brainstorming format is especially appropriate for seeking ideas for peace. Usually when people speak, they feel that they own their ideas and must defend them. When people who have differences speak, each tries to win over the other. The result is that there are winners and losers, and nobody wants to be a loser. There is a better way—brainstorming—so that ideas belong to the group, not to individuals. A technique used to encourage creative thinking, brainstorming is a way to generate as many ideas as possible with the assumption that they can later be evaluated, developed, and acted upon.

A few principles of brainstorming are listed here.

(1) Define the problem you are discussing before you begin. It is better to do it in a general format and to make sure that the definition is not itself a solution. You are trying to brainstorm

ways of achieving goals. You want your goals to be clearly understood and to some extent limited, even though you don't want to start out limiting the means for reaching them.

(2) Generate a large number of ideas. The larger the initial list, the more good ideas you will have after you evaluate them. One idea can suggest another. It is best at the early stage to have as many ideas as possible.

(3) Avoid criticizing ideas and owning ideas. Ideas, once suggested, are the property of everyone. Brainstorming is a collective activity. If people feel that they will be judged for their ideas, they become inhibited.

(4) Give everyone an opportunity to participate. It is disastrous for a brainstorming session if only a few people participate because the group is robbed of the creative talents of those who are excluded. The best results occur when everyone participates.

(5) Record all ideas. It is useful to have a collective memory. Recording ideas serves several important purposes: it lets people know that their ideas matter—after all, they are recorded; it lets the group see what has already been said, so people do not repeat the same things again and again; and, it frees participants from worrying about remembering their ideas— ideas are owned by the collective memory.

(6) Make the role of conference moderator clear. The moderator keeps the process going and aims toward the goal of getting useful suggestions. This person is not a participant and should not impose views upon the group. The moderator controls the process but not the result. The moderator's function is to elicit responses from the group, encourage participation by all members, and protect members from criticism—not to judge, teach, dominate, or try to control the outcome in any way, except to ensure that the group stays on task. The suggestions that come from the brainstorming session are those of the group's participants.

(7) Make the recorder's role clear. The recorder writes down every suggestion made by the participants, using a large pad so that all can see them being recorded. This person should be objective and have the ability to listen, to comprehend the main point, and to summarize accurately any consensus reached. Between sessions the recorder must work to write a summary of suggestions in order to report what the group has agreed on.

(8) Have specific questions related to working for peace, such as "How can we produce leaders who will work for peace?" It is useful to prepare worksheets to help conference participants keep on task.

Sample Brainstorming Worksheet

Below is a worksheet for a conference on Producing Leaders Who Will Work for Peace. It is adapted from an actual conference on Producing Leaders Who Will Consider the Future which was conducted by the Tallahassee Future Society.

PEACE CONFERENCE WORKSHEET

THEME: How can we produce leaders who will work for peace?

GROUP SESSION I: ANALYSIS OF THE PROBLEM: What factors inhibit leadership for peace?

1. Do the attitudes and values of citizens discourage leaders from pursuing peace?
2. How well do we prepare political leaders to lead for peace?
3. Do governmental processes inhibit leadership for peace?

GROUP SESSION II: IDENTIFICATION OF SOLUTIONS: What factors would encourage leadership for peace?

1. How can citizens encourage leadership for peace?
2. How can we best prepare those attracted to political leadership to lead for peace?
3. What changes can we make in the governmental process to maximize leadership for peace?

Thinking of Positive Steps for Peace

We must not lose our ability to think of positive alternatives. Think of the most desirable outcome and ask what we must do to achieve it. There is no guarantee that we can achieve the most optimistic goals, but without positive goals, we are doomed to an undesirable path. In appendix B, I report on the results of a brainstorming session on thinking of positive steps for peace.

Dare to dream. Imagine a world without war. Societies move toward that which they envision. List your hopes of the best things that could happen. The military planners are continually trying to imagine the worst scenarios. Those who want peace should be aware of dangers but not let those dangers keep them from imagining the best possibilities.

Imagine an escalation of goodwill between the United States and the Soviet Union. There could be one, just as there was an escalation of mistrust during the arms race. The rule of the arms race was that actions were returned in kind. The same would hold true for acts of goodwill, and we might think of ways to create such an escalation.

It is not utopian to think that people in the United States and the Soviet Union and all the other nations will get tired of war and begin to plan for peace. Those who think that the world can survive with nuclear weapons and arms escalations are the unrealistic dreamers. It is not unrealistic to think that people will choose life over death.

Imagine a world at peace in the year 2010. It would not be a society without conflicts, because conflict is inevitable, but it would be a world in which people resolve their conflicts without violence. Imagine what that society would be like, and the methods people would use to resolve conflict. Then work backwards to imagine how the people of that society might have abolished war. Trace that future society back to the present time. List the specific things they had to do by the year 2010 to create a nonviolent world. That will give you an idea of what we must do.

We do not achieve every goal that we desire, but we do not ever achieve goals without first desiring them. Try to envision a desirable world. The greatest poverty in the world today is a poverty of vision. In other ages, people dreamed of utopias and those dreams fostered social change. Since World War II, people have thought in terms of distopia—avoiding the worst possibility—and we have been approaching that worst possibility by building more weapons. We need to think of positive goals in order to have a positive future.

19

■ ■ ■

Deciding What to Do

■ ■ ■

The most important thing in working for peace is to choose actions that can bring about the desired results. In this chapter I discuss alternative philosophies on how to work for peace, how to choose between them, and the implications of our choice for actual decisions we must make. I begin by reviewing the choices presented in this book and conclude with a discussion of how the choice we make can guide our reactions to events such as the Persian Gulf War.

Alternative Approaches to Peace

I have discussed many different approaches to working for peace in this book. In Part I, working to end particular wars was contrasted with working to abolish war. Those who want to work for peace have to decide whether to define peace as the removal of conflict or whether to seek the minimum requirements for resolving conflicts between nations.

In Part II, alternative institutional structures for settling conflicts between nations were explored. We can support nations giving up little bits of their sovereignty in well-defined areas as is being done in the European Community, or we can work for a world federation analogous to the United States. Some groups believe a federation might come from reforming the United Nations, while others want to create a new international organization.

In Part III, options related to security were examined. The United States might seek military superiority or accept that no one can win wars in the nuclear age. We might accept deterrence or try to replace it, either with the Strategic Defense Initiative or by abolishing war. Our most important choice is whether to continue to rely on national defense or whether to replace national defense with common security.

In Part IV, military alliances were contrasted with common security. Security in Europe after German unification and the continuing of both arms reductions and reform in the Soviet Union are tied in with the issue of establishing a system of common security in Europe, either through the European Community or through the United Nations.

In Part V, global education that fosters a planetary consciousness was contrasted with nationalistic education. We might support or reject the concept of global education and we might accept or reject the claim that peace studies, more specifically studies in conflict resolution and game theory, make a contribution to peace.

I do not pretend that I have covered all the ways of working for peace. In aiming our efforts I think we should try to aim as directly as possible at the problem of war. Many approaches move in the right direction, but not all come close to the target. I tried to choose the methods of working for peace that I thought were aimed most directly. No doubt many other approaches make important contributions to peace.

Choosing an Approach

We need to do some serious thinking about avoiding a nuclear holocaust. Such thinking involves defining the problem and examining alternative solutions that have been proposed. Those who are serious about working for peace must engage in the critical process of separating what makes sense from what does not.

Peace activists should debate how we should direct our efforts. The idea of debate, of argumentation, of critical examination, is thought by some to be foreign to the idea of peace. Within the peace movement many individuals do not like to confront others and their ideas. They assume a definition of peace that precludes conflict. But conflicting views of how to work for peace exist, and if we are to be effective we must have discussion and consciously decide between viewpoints.

I have written this book to help the process of debating ways to work for peace. I hope that some of its readers are activists who will discuss the viewpoints contained here. To help structure a discussion of the points raised, I have included discussion questions for each chapter in appendix C.

How can you know that doing certain things will bring about a peaceful world? Imagine that a program of action has a following large enough to be effective. Then see whether its being followed would establish peace. For example, suppose that people committed to world peace through world law were to establish a base with local peace groups throughout the country. And suppose that these groups were to help elect leaders who are committed to enforceable international law. Suppose also that leaders in other nations were committed to world peace through world law. If this point were reached, and we established enforceable world law, war would be abolished.

If one believes that we can abolish war by instituting enforced international law, then that belief leads to advocating certain actions. Unlike people who believe that we need to transform human nature and work for that transformation, advocates of world peace through world law try to change institutions.

Crises as Opportunities

The world faces many crises that are also opportunities to help establish enforced international law. Instead of despairing, we might build institutions that not only solve the problem at hand but also establish international law. By this process we can work for the abolition of war. Many problems, including the environmental crisis, regional conflicts between nations, and conflicts soon to develop over the oceans and outer space, can be solved only by strengthening international law.

The environmental crisis is our most visible problem. We can see it and all too often even smell it. The nuclear threat is not as obvious—one does not experience the danger of nuclear weapons until it is too late, a fact that has led some people to believe that we would have to experience another exchange of nuclear weapons before taking action. Now we have a visible crisis that can only be solved on a global level. The earth is warming. Emissions must be reduced. The rain forests must be protected.

Because environmental problems transcend national boundaries, it makes sense to have a World Environmental Agency. Sulfur emissions in the United States cause acid rain in Canada, and emissions in the Ruhr valley of Germany cause acid rain in Sweden. We cannot solve environmental problems on the national level. Successful attempts to limit pollution will involve international cooperation. A first step would be the creation of a supranational research institute on the environment that would monitor levels of pollutants worldwide. Global institutions must be strengthened to deal with this immediate problem, and those institutions will aid in the abolition of war.

In several areas of the world conflicts threaten to involve other nations. The Iran-Iraq war spilled beyond those countries and involved bombing ships from third countries. Wars fought by any nations can endanger other nations, so the world community has an interest in controlling conflict.

A proposal for UN security forces that would help in areas of conflict has been formulated by a conference of experts, including the former commanders of UN forces in Lebanon, the Congo, and the Sinai.[4] Currently, the United Nations uses forces from neutral countries on an ad hoc basis. These experts, who have commanded UN peacekeeping forces, advocate the establishment of a reserve of armed forces for UN service with a permanent core staff. These forces could be used at the call of a country that feared aggression and be put in place before aggression took place.

We may soon face the possibility of wars over exploration rights in the ocean. When the United Nations was founded, drilling for oil could only occur at a depth of seventy feet; now it can occur at several hundred feet. Today there are conflicting claims to oil reserves in many areas, including the South China Sea, where Taiwan, China, Japan, and South Korea all have claims. A solution to conflict over the oceans would be to place under UN sovereignty the two-thirds of the earth's surface that is water. The UN could regulate and tax exploration in the oceans, which, besides preventing war over exploration rights, would provide the UN with an independent source of income.

Space can be a frontier for peace or a frontier for war. Right now we are preparing to make space another battlefield. If this occurs it will become possible to attack satellites, and then it will be impossible to use satellites to verify arms control agreements. If we act soon enough, we can easily create a verifiable disarmament agreement covering space. Such a treaty could include public inspection of all space cargo payloads, and, because anyone with a telescope can tell when something is put into space, a treaty would be entirely verifiable.

Each of these crises is also an opportunity to strengthen international law. If we acted on the suggestions for solving each of these problems we would not only help the problem at hand but we would also help build the international order needed to handle other problems.

Building a Movement to Abolish War

To succeed, the movement to outlaw war must become a mass movement. The issue of abolishing war must be brought before the public. The easiest way to do this is for those who support world peace through world law to transform antiwar movements into a peace movement that seeks the abolition of war.

In building respect for international law it is not enough that nations conform to international law. Nations must end illegal wars because they violate international laws. This is analogous to Immanuel Kant's dictum that it is not enough to act in accord with duty—we must act out of a sense of duty, because one of our goals is that people be motivated by certain factors. When we are clear that we are acting because it is the right thing to do, we make it more likely that others will also act from the same sense of duty. If nations act out of a respect for international law, they make it more likely that others will also act from a sense of duty. Those who favor outlawing war must make it a duty to respect international law.

Means and ends cannot be separated, because one of our ends is that people use certain means. Each time we act we are choosing the type of world we want to have. The means used are part of the end result and should be judged according to whether it is desirable that people use those means in the future. If people want the means of law to be used in ending conflicts between nations, they should cite support for international law as the motive of their actions.

U.S. Interventions

It would have been better if more people who demonstrated to end the illegal actions of the United States against Nicaragua had carried signs that showed support for international law. Nicaragua had sued the United States and won in the International Court of

Justice. The court held that "the United States had violated international law by interfering, through the use of force, with the internal affairs of a sovereign nation. . . . U.S. actions in training, equipping, financing, and supplying the contra forces was a violation of international law."[5] The United States refused to recognize the jurisdiction of the court—a clear case of ignoring international law. Nicaragua had taken its case, as any nation should take its complaints, to the international court, and the United States had claimed that it was not bound by the court's decision. The battle lines for supporting international law were clearly drawn.

People in each country can begin the task of working for peace by making sure that the leaders of their country respect international law, or by replacing those leaders with ones who will. Several actions of the United States have worked to weaken international law, however desirable the other goals attained by these actions. The United States was in violation of international law in its invasions of Grenada and Panama and was criticized by the United Nations for both these actions. In our invasion of Panama we did much more than capture President Manuel Noriega. We also killed over two hundred innocent civilians and weakened respect for international law. Iraq's Saddam Hussein mentioned the invasions of Grenada and Panama in his attempt to justify Iraq's invasion of Kuwait.

Iraq's Invasion of Kuwait

As with many other crises, Iraq's invasion of Kuwait on August 2, 1990, provided an opportunity to show support for international law. All members of the United Nations should come to the aid of any member that is attacked. In passing over a dozen resolutions calling first for an embargo of Iraq, and then authorizing the use of force, the UN actions showed that the nations of the world can work together.

U.S. involvement in the Persian Gulf War touched on two different commitments, first to Saudi Arabia because the United States has a military treaty with that country, and second to the charter of the United Nations. Troops were initially sent to Saudi Arabia to fulfill treaty obligations and not because the United Nations requested that we send troops. UN actions at first were limited to passing resolutions that established an embargo of Iraq.

Because Iraq is dependent on exports of oil and imports of food, it was thought that an embargo might be sufficient to induce Iraq to withdraw from Kuwait.

The two different actions by the United States—sending troops to Saudi Arabia and supporting the embargo of Iraq—were based on two different security systems, the system of military alliances and the system of common security. Before the invasion, the United States let Saddam Hussein know that it did not have a military alliance with Kuwait and neglected to mention that it would support UN action to meet aggression against any nation. If the United States had made its commitment to the concept of common security as clear as it made its commitment to military pacts, Iraq might not have invaded.

The U.S. build-up in Saudi Arabia confused the clear UN message for international law and it transformed the international community's unified response to Iraq's aggression into a confrontation between the United States and Iraq. Thus while Iran supported the embargo it opposed the deployment of U.S. troops in Saudi Arabia.

The United Nations voted on November 29, 1990, to give sanctions until January 15, 1991, to work, and authorized the use of force after that date. On January 17, "Desert Storm," a campaign of twenty-eight allied nations, began. Using a new generation of weapons, including Stealth aircraft that are invisible to radar, sea-launched cruise missiles, and smart bombs, the allied forces were able to destroy Iraq's air defenses within hours. With almost complete air supremacy, allied aircraft bombed Iraq continuously for thirty-eight days before starting a ground war that was complete in a hundred hours. The war ended when Iraq accepted the UN resolutions, agreeing to recognize Kuwait's independence and pay for the damage the invasion had caused.

On the day the ground war began, President Bush in a televised address outlined the aims of the war and a vision of a new world order. He said,

> This is a historic moment. We have in this past year made great progress in ending the long era of conflict and cold war. We have before us the opportunity to forge for ourselves and for future generations a new world order, a world where the rule of law, not the law of the jungle, governs the conduct of nations.
>
> When we are successful, and we will be, we will have a real chance

at this new world order, an order in which a credible United Nations can use its peacekeeping role to fulfill the promise and vision of the UN's founders.[6]

Those who want to work for peace need to be involved in defining what the new world order will be. One possibility is to have the United States act as the world's policeman—a Pax America similar to the Pax Romana of the ancient world. The analysis of this book favors the alternative vision of a UN World Federation of equal nations that would apply international law impartially.

The Persian Gulf war demonstrates what needs to be done to establish international law. We need to have a permanent UN peacekeeping force. If additional troops are required, they need to serve under a UN command. Decisions of the United Nations, such as the decision to have an embargo of Iraq, must be binding on all nations. Nations must use and respect the decisions of international courts, so that accusations such as those that Iraq made against Kuwait—of stealing oil by slant drilling—can be settled in court. The United Nations must have agencies for verification of arms control, and regional systems of common security within a global system of common security must be established. All weapons of mass destruction must be banned.

Everything that happens is not for the best, but we are wise to make the best of everything that happens. Peace activists should use every crisis as an opportunity to strengthen international law. The Persian Gulf War has people thinking about a new world order in which obedience to international law is the rule. To justify our actions we did not mention our desire for cheap oil, or our wanting to keep undemocratic governments in power—we mentioned respect for international law and support for the United Nations. These slogans will help guide our future actions.

When we compare the world's reaction to Iraq's invasion of Kuwait with the reaction to Italy's invasion of Ethiopia more than fifty years ago, we see that some progress has been made toward international law. The League of Nations disbanded because nations were not able to unite against aggression. This time nations have united. During the 1990s, the UN's Decade of International Law, we could make enforced international law a reality. When that happens, we will have abolished war.

Appendix A

■ ■ ■

Peace Center Committees and Activities

■ ■ ■

You can accomplish more working for peace if you work with others. Here you will find a list of committees from a community peace organization—the Tallahassee Peace Coalition in Tallahassee, Florida. This will give you an idea of some of the things you might do for peace by working with a community organization.

Things that can be done for peace are listed here according to categories. Your local group might have committees for each type of activity. If you don't have enough members in your local group to form separate committees, you might still use this list as a guide for dividing tasks among the members you do have. Even individuals working alone can use this list to get ideas of things to do.

Details of each committee's work are provided. In each case the main purpose of the committee is listed, followed by a list of activities that you might become involved in. The first three committees—membership, running the office, and fundraising—are essential to keeping the peace center going, while the last three functions—community outreach, networking, and political action—are more directly related to working for peace.

Membership Commitee

Purpose: To encourage more people to join the peace center, to encourage those who have joined to become active, to bring people together at regular meetings, and to help build a supportive environment for individuals seeking peace.

Activities

1. Invite individuals who express an interest in working for peace to monthly meetings, seminars, and committee meetings, according to their interests.
2. Help people get started working for peace by explaining the committee structure so they can see where they might fit in.
3. Telephone new and inactive members to describe activities and invite individuals to participate on some level.
4. Sponsor regular parties—picnics, living room dialogues, block parties, beach parties—so that members can get to know each other.
5. Plan a program for each monthly general meeting.
6. Provide refreshments and supplies for a pot-luck dessert at each monthly general meeting. Provide and plan for clean-up after meetings and provide child care during meetings.

Running the Office

Purpose: To provide a home for the peace center, to coordinate and carry out activities and programs, to provide a convenient place for public contact, and to provide educational resources on peace issues.

Activities

1. Help keep the office open at regular hours by volunteering to spend time in the office.
2. Prepare for events and programs.
3. Help put out the newsletter every month by writing, typing, collating, stapling, or helping to mail it out.
4. Inventory, catalog, and order library materials.
5. Order and sell bulk literature items.
6. Keep the files up to date on peace activities.
7. Speak with individuals who come to the office.

Fundraising

Purpose: To secure financial resources necessary for the peace center to continue its peace education activities.

Activities

1. Compile a portfolio showing the peace center's history and accomplishments.
2. Show a portfolio on the peace center to people sympathetic to the cause of peace as a means of attracting donations.
3. Research foundations that might fund special programs.
4. Have benefits such as dinners, concerts, films, and auctions.
5. Ask members of the peace center to become contributing members who give a set amount each month.
6. Maintain a tax-exempt peace educational trust that helps to support the educational activities of the peace center and approach potential donors personally.

Community Outreach

Purpose: To establish links to the local community and to specific organizations to provide information on selected peace issues.

Activities

1. Hold educational workshops on the nuclear arms race.
2. Counsel people as needed on the draft and conscientious objection.
3. Counsel people regarding conscientious objection to paying tax money for weapons and war.
4. Prepare press releases.
5. Encourage peace education on all levels, including public and private primary, secondary, and postsecondary schools. Help institute peace studies programs at the university level.
6. Maintain contact with other groups in the community, being sure to omit no segment of the population.
7. Keep a list of speakers who can make presentations to community groups. Conduct training sessions to prepare speakers.
8. Provide resources for presentations, such as flip charts on the nuclear arms race and information packets on selected issues.
9. Prepare peace education materials, such as multimedia presentations, displays, and materials that can be used in the schools.
10. Conduct essay contests aimed at getting people of different ages to think about peace-related issues.

Movement Building

Purpose: To make people conscious of the dangers to survival that we all face, build a sense of planetary citizenship, and create an awareness of the need to work together to avoid those dangers.

Activities

1. Maintain correspondence with other peace movements throughout the United States and in other countries.
2. Initiate cultural, athletic, and educational exchanges with people of other countries.
3. Promote friendship through sister city programs whereby cities in the United States are paired with cities in other countries.
4. Promote the learning of Esperanto as an international language, until such time as a better language for this purpose is devised.
5. Sponsor public speakers and public symposiums.

Political Action

Purpose: To actively support individuals and organizations that share its goal of ending the nuclear arms race and establishing world peace through world law.

Activities

1. Monitor legislation on all levels that bears on the quest for peace.
2. Maintain a telephone tree to implement legislative alerts that inform members of important legislation so that they can contact their elected representatives.
3. Maintain a mail alert to write to representatives expressing the views of the membership.
4. Collect signatures on petitions.
5. Endorse political candidates.

Appendix B

■ ■ ■

Brainstorming Positive Steps for Peace

■ ■ ■

This list was the result of a brainstorming session on how to work for peace. Eight people attended this session and represented varied backgrounds. We asked what each of the following can do for peace: individuals, local groups, schools and universities, churches, local governments, state governments, and national governments. We also examined what can be negotiated between nations. This is what the participants listed. The suggestions were not evaluated and none were eliminated.

Individuals

1. Let people know that you are concerned.
2. Educate yourself on world affairs.
3. Read good newspapers, get access to international news and the international press.
4. Listen to shortwave radio to hear international news.
5. Contact local, state, national, and international leaders to let them know your views.
6. Write letters to newspapers.
7. Refuse to participate in the military.

Local Groups

1. Keep watch on issues to contact people about.
2. Send out mass mailings and provide preaddressed postcards to make it easier for people to write elected officials.

3. Help people express support for unilateral arms reduction and unilateral initiatives for peace.
4. Get endorsements from respected local leaders. Try to involve people who are respected in the community.
5. Encourage peace-minded individuals to run for public office.
6. Support tax and draft resisters.

Schools and Universities

1. Provide multicultural education.
2. Have instruction on conflict resolution.
3. Provide expertise in analyzing problems related to peace.
4. Offer courses on topics related to peace.

Churches

1. Form Peace Task Forces to educate membership by means of a peace-oriented curriculum.
2. Lead petition drives for such positive goals as a freeze on nuclear weapons.
3. Promote values that help peace.
4. Combat antipeace theologies and support pro-peace theologies. Antipeace theologies include the view that nuclear war is part of God's plan. Propeace theologies include the view that humans have no right to destroy God's creation—the destruction of the Earth is the ultimate blasphemy.
5. Help combat the fatalism that makes many people feel helpless.
6. Promote individual responsibility.
7. Provide hope for change.

Local Governments

1. Vote for resolutions declaring themselves nuclear free zones.
2. Pass a resolution enabling the local community to become a sister city with a community in the Soviet Union. This can involve official declarations and exchange programs.
3. Display the United Nations flag at city hall.
4. Encourage peace-minded individuals to enter politics.

State Level

1. Pass resolutions for unilateral steps that the United States might take for peace.
2. Refuse to allow the placement of missiles in the state.
3. Initiate plans for conversion of military-industrial plants to peaceful use to minimize economic disruption.
4. Monitor international business conducted by firms based in the state to insure that they are dealing fairly and ethically with other peoples. Many states have foreign affairs departments that could set and monitor standards.
5. End civil defense planning for nuclear war. Refuse to go along with the farce of pretending that a nuclear war is survivable.

National Level

1. Reduce troop strength abroad.
2. Take unilateral initiatives for peace.
3. Do away with draft registration.
4. Insure that the United States is fair in dealings with other nations. Examine the ethics of our dealings.
5. Apply the same safety standards to foreign sales that are applied to domestic sales. Do not allow companies to dump unsafe products abroad.
6. Allow alternative service in place of military service.
7. Allow payment into an alternative peace tax fund in place of spending money on the military.
8. Support the United Nations.

Negotiated Between Nations

1. Allow individuals to declare themselves world citizens, exempt from national conscription and bound to pay taxes to a world authority rather than a nation state. The number of such citizens who take this option on each side can be balanced through negotiation.
2. Begin massive exchange programs involving millions of citizens who would visit each other's country.
3. Provide television and radio time for an international debate among all the peoples of the world to hasten the process of forming an international consensus on issues that divide people.

4. Create a joint U.S.-USSR university and create student exchange programs.
5. Support peace academies that are truly international and free from any national control.
6. Negotiate an end to defamation of each other's people in the media in the same way that the civil rights movement was able to fight the defamation of minorities in the media.
7. Internationalize the oceans and outer space.
8. Create nuclear free zones in Europe, the Middle East, Africa, and other areas.
9. Allow peace activists to form independent organizations so that there would be independent peace organizations in both the United States and the USSR.

Appendix C

■ ■ ■

Discussion Questions by Chapters

■ ■ ■

Chapter 1: What Does the Peace Movement Offer?

1. Are there differences between a peace movement and an anti-war movement? If so, then what are some of the differences?
2. Judge these actions according to whether those outside the peace movement can easily understand the purpose of the action: pointing out waste in military spending and supporting steps to strengthen the United Nations.
3. Think of actions taken by peace groups and judge those actions according to how effective you think they are, using as a criterion of effectiveness how well people outside the peace movement can understand those actions.
4. Write a short description of the type of peace movement that you would like to have exist.
5. What actions can a peace movement take that would present an alternative to the system of war?

Chapter 2: Defining Peace

1. What is wrong with defining peace as "disarmament"?
2. What is wrong with defining peace as "ending all conflicts"?
3. What are the differences between removing, reducing, and resolving conflicts?
4. Contrast the idealist and the materialist view of human conflict.

5. Are we at peace or are we at war? State definitions of war and peace in your answer to this question.

Chapter 3: Resolving Conflicts without Violence

1. What factor does Emery Reves believe is always present where there is peace and always lacking where there is war?
2. How might you test the relationship between submitting disputes to arbitration and the onset of war?
3. When did castles in Europe become obsolete and why did they become obsolete?
4. State John Locke's argument that concludes that people should accept a common authority to judge their conflicts. What happens if people do not have a common judge?
5. Explain what Thomas Hobbes means by authority and how by accepting an authority (arbiter, representative, or sovereign) a multitude of persons is made one person.

Chapter 4: The Alternative to War

1. According to Margaret Mead, when is it possible to replace a social invention, such as war?
2. What social invention can replace war?
3. In what ways is the analogy between the Articles of Confederation and the United Nations strong, and in which ways is the analogy weak?
4. Would George Washington want to strengthen the United Nations or to replace it with a stronger international organization? Are arguments that he made in favor of strengthening the bond among the thirteen colonies relevant to the United Nations?
5. Supposing that the nations of the world move towards a federal system of world order, which model do you think they would be more likely to use: the U.S. model or the European Community model?

Chapter 5: Organizations Working to Outlaw War

1. Describe some of the things the United Nations does. What has been the attitude of the United States towards the United Nations?
2. Explain the federalist principle and what it means to add another level of government, as world federalists advocate.

3. List five things that the Campaign for United Nations Reform advocates as ways of strengthening the United Nations. What effect would these actions have?
4. Contrast the World Federalist Association with the American Movement for World Government and the World Constitution and Parliament Association. How do these organizations differ in their approach?
5. How much progress has there really been toward the goal of outlawing war?

Chapter 6: Objections to the Proposal to Outlaw War

1. What do you think are the biggest obstacles to world federalism?
2. Explain the idea that a nation can protect its citizens. Do nations assume that this is true? Is it true?
3. Explain the idea that a nation can act as judge of its conflicts with other nations. Do nations assume that this is possible?
4. Explain the idea that a nation can be sovereign in international affairs. Do nations assume that this is true? Is it a sensible idea?
5. Is there any real hope that the United States and the Soviet Union could agree on disarmament?

Chapter 7: Military Advantage in the Nucear Age

1. Why did the United States drop the atomic bomb on Japan?
2. Why did the arms race occur?
3. What has been true in the past regarding claims of weapons gaps between the United States and the Soviet Union? Cite examples.
4. Did the United States win the Cuban missile crisis? Back your answer with facts about what happened.
5. What will happen as more and more nations get atomic weapons?

Chapter 8: Deterrence and the Strategic Defense Initiative

1. Explain the strategy of deterrence.
2. What is the difference between strategic and tactical weapons?

3. State the criteria by which wars might be judged just or unjust according to the just war tradition.
4. State arguments in favor of having a tactical defense rather than a strategic defense system.
5. Can the Strategic Defense Initiative work? Can it make us more secure?

Chapter 9: From National Defense to Common Security

1. How dangerous is our world?
2. Describe the types of agreements that have been reached.
3. How does the Strategic Defense Initiative relate to agreements that have been reached or that might be reached?
4. Why is it incorrect to label the nuclear freeze proposal a Soviet idea and the Stategic Defense Initiative an American idea?
5. Why might it seem hypocritical to people in the Soviet Union that the United States now rejects a nuclear weapons freeze?

Chapter 10: Why the U.S. and the USSR Need Common Security

1. Describe the changes that have occurred in the Soviet Union. Are these changes substantial or just superficial?
2. Describe the changes that have occurred in Eastern Europe.
3. Contrast common security with security through alliances.
4. How is common security versus alliances tied in with German unification and the independence movements in various Soviet republics?
5. What are some incentives of the Soviet Union and of the United States for embracing common security?

Chapter 11: American Soviet Citizen Diplomacy

1. Read the resolution of the Tallahassee City Commission that invited the city of Krasnodar in the Soviet Union to be Tallahassee's sister city. What objections could there be to passing such a resolution?
2. What if a sister city in the Soviet Union sent only officials to the United States instead of ordinary citizens? Would the program be worthless in such a case?

3. In visiting the Soviet Union on a goodwill mission, should you visit dissidents who are trying to get out of the Soviet Union or is that impolite to your hosts?
4. Is it any of our business how the government of the Soviet Union treats its citizens?
5. Try to envision a goodwill escalation replacing the arms race. What might it be like?

Chapter 12: American and Soviet Philosophers Discuss Peace

1. Can modern warfare be just?
2. Who is to blame for the arms race?
3. Is conflict inevitable due to differences on human rights?
4. What can be done to ease tensions?
5. Would you like to discuss issues related to peace with people from around the world? What issues would you like to discuss? Is there anything in particular you would want to say?

Chapter 13: Developing Planetary Citizens

1. What can increased communications do?
2. What are problems, prospects, and alternatives to having English as an international language?
3. How can global consciousness be increased?
4. How can people learn to be fair and open minded?
5. What methods can be used to help create acceptance of a group as an international authority? What did Amnesty International do to protect their credibility?

Chapter 14: Peace Studies and Research Centers

1. Examine a history textbook and judge whether it is written from a global perspective.
2. What is the difference between concentrating on the causes of particular wars and concentrating on the cause of war? Will the first lead to the second?
3. What is uniquely peace studies?
4. What aspects of traditional education might be considered especially relevant to peace?
5. How does our ability to perceive reality relate to peace?

Chapter 15: Lessons in Conflict Resolution and Game Theory

1. Contrast interests and issues. Think of examples where people disagree on issues but agree on interests.
2. Contrast competition, compromise, and collaboration.
3. Describe in detail what a successful mediator does in a mediation session.
4. Describe some research in conflict resolution and how we might use the results in the pursuit of peace.
5. Describe the prisoner's dilemma. Is there a solution to the prisoner's dilemma?

Chapter 16: Doing Your Share for Peace

1. Why might people think that we will annihilate ourselves?
2. Can you know whether we can succeed in abolishing war? Would it be worthwhile to try even if we cannot succeed? Can we succeed?
3. How can you respond to the claim that "If you don't have a lot of people our efforts will be wasted and if you have a lot of people then you won't need me. So either my efforts will be wasted or you won't need me"?
4. How do alert networks function? Discuss both mail and phone alerts.
5. Contrast what can be done in fifteen minutes a week with what can be done by spending an hour a week working for peace.

Chapter 17: Working for Peace in Your Community

1. What is the importance of local peace groups? Why can't we just have national organizations?
2. How might national peace organizations interact with local groups to benefit both?
3. What are some problems that local peace groups face and how might they solve these problems?
4. What does planning for success involve in relation to peace groups?
5. Using the marketing model, who is the client that peace groups must please? How can peace groups be more successful according to the marketing model?

Chapter 18: Brainstorming Ways to Work for Peace

1. What is brainstorming?
2. What is the role of the mediator in a brainstorming session?
3. What is the role of the recorder in a brainstorming session?
4. What are the stages of a brainstorming session?
5. Design a brainstorming session to think of ways of working for peace for a group in your community. Have the group work on a specific aspect of working for peace.

Chapter 19: Deciding What to Do

1. What view do you hold on some of the alternative approaches to peace? Do you think that peace involves the removal of conflict or just the resolution of conflict? What type of institutional structures, if any, might be needed for peace? What do you think of deterrence and the Strategic Defense Initiative, and of common security and military alliances? What do you think peace education should include?
2. Have you changed any opinions as a result of this book? If so, what was your opinion and why did you change it?
3. Do you think that an atomic bomb will be used again before people will be willing to abolish war? Defend your answer.
4. Name a crisis that is also an opportunity to work to strengthen international law. Explain how the crisis is also an opportunity.
5. State how you would handle a contemporary crisis and the viewpoint on how to work for peace that would guide your action.

Notes

Part I: Thinking about Peace

1. Gottfried Wilhelm Freiherr von Leibniz, *Leibniz Selections,* ed. Philip P. Weiner (New York: Charles Scribner's Sons, 1951), p. 24.
2. Ibid., p. 25
3. Thomas Hobbes, *Leviathan,* ed. Michael Oakeschott (London: Collier Macmillan Publishers, 1962), p. 100.
4. Emery Reves, *The Anatomy of Peace* (New York: Harper & Brothers, 1945; Gloucester, Mass.: Peter Smith, 1969), p. 121.
5. Ibid.
6. Ibid., pp. 121–22.
7. Peter H. Rohn, *Treaty Profiles* (Santa Barbara, Calif.: Cleo Press, 1976), p. 8.
8. Gregory A. Raymond, *Conflict Resolution and the Structure of the State System: An Analysis of Arbitrative Settlement* (Montclair, N.J.: Allen Osmun & Company, 1980), pp. 98, 83.
9. A.M. Stuyt, *Survey of International Arbitrations, 1794–1970* (Leiden: A.W. Sijhoff, 1972).
10. Raymond, *Conflict Resolution,* p. 95.
11. John Locke, *Two Treatises of Government: A Critical Edition with an Introduction and Apparatus Criticus by Peter Laslett* (Cambridge: Cambridge University Press, 1967), p. 298.
12. David W. Felder, *The Relationship of Fact, Value, and Obligation in Hobbes's Leviathan* (Ann Arbor: University Microfilms International, 1978).

13. Hobbes, *Leviathan,* p. 127.
14. Ibid., p. 202.
15. Locke, *Two Treatises,* p. 300.

Part 2: Outlawing War

1. Margaret Mead, "Warfare Is Only an Invention—Not a Biological Necessity," in *Peace and War,* ed. Charles R. Beitz and Theodore Herman (San Francisco: W.H. Freeman, 1973), pp. 112–18.
2. Karl von Clausewitz, *On War,* ed. Anatol Rapoport (New York: Penguin, 1968), p. 119.
3. Norman Cousins, "The First and the Finest," *The Economist,* 28 February–6 March 1987, p. 19.
4. Catherine Drinker Bowen, *Miracle at Philadelphia: The Story of the Constitutional Convention May to September 1787* (Boston: Little, Brown and Company, 1966), p. 88.
5. Edward Conrad Smith, ed., *The Constitution of the United States* (New York: Barnes and Noble, 1979), p. 6.
6. Clarence Streit, *Union Now* (New York: Harper & Brothers, 1940), p. 33.
7. Tom A. Hudgens, *Let's Abolish War* (Denver, Colo.: BILR Corporation, 1985), p. 42.
8. Barbara M. Walker, ed., *The World Federalist Bicentennial Reader* (Washington, D.C.: World Federalist Association, 1987), p. 4.
9. Bowen, *Miracle at Philadelphia,* p. 89.
10. Arthur Holcombe, *One More Perfect Union* (Cambridge: Harvard University Press, 1950), p. 2.
11. Max Farrand, ed., *Records of the Federal Convention of 1787,* (New Haven: Yale University Press, 1937), 1:464.
12. Ibid., p. 515.
13. This famous speech was given on September 19, 1946, in Zurich.
14. Abba Eban, "The Palestinian Problem—A New Approach," *New Outlook,* Vol. 23, No. 1.
15. John Pinder, in the *World Federalist Bicentennial Reader* (Washington, D.C.: World Federalist Association, 1987), p. 95.
16. Ibid.
17. *World Federalist: Newsmagazine of the World Federalist Association,* 7, no. 4 (December 1982): 2.

18. Alliance for Our Common Future, c/o National Peace Institute Foundation, 110 Maryland Avenue, N.E., Washington, D.C. 20002, (202) 546-9500.
19. Steve Dimoff, United Nations Association, (202) 347-5004.
20. Roper Organization poll conducted March 11 and 18, 1989, with 1,978 in-person, at-home interviews.
21. John Austin, "The Province of Jurisprudence Determined," in *The Austinian Conception of Law,* ed. Jethro Brown (London: John Murray, 1838), pp. 20, 19.
22. Roger Fisher, *International Conflict for Beginners* (New York: Harper Torchbooks, 1969), p. 154.
23. David W. Felder, "Command Theory and International Law," *Philosophy Forum,* 15 (1977): 299–306.
24. House Concurrent Resolution 123: Common security—a blueprint for survival," *Congressional Record,* 98th Cong., 1st sess. (Washington, D.C.: U.S. Government Printing Office), May 10, 1983.

Part 3: Providing Security

1. R. H. Ferrell, ed., *Off the Record: The Private Papers of Harry S. Truman* (New York: Harper and Row, 1980), p. 53.
2. U.S. Department of State, *Foreign Relations: Conference of Berlin (Potsdam) 1945,* 2 vols. (Washington, D.C.: U.S. Government Printing Office, 1960), 2:460.
3. Dwight D. Eisenhower, *The White House Years: Mandate for Change, 1953–1956* (Garden City, N.Y.: Doubleday, 1963), pp. 312–13; W. D. Leahy, *I Was There: The Personal Story of the Chief of Staff to Presidents Roosevelt and Truman, Based on His Notes and Diaries Made at the Time* (New York: Whittlesey House, 1950), pp. 439–42.
4. Herbert Feis, *Churchill–Roosevelt–Stalin: The War They Waged and the Peace They Sought* (Princeton: Princeton University Press, 1957), pp. 450–51.
5. U.S. Department of State, *Foreign Relations,* 1: 358.
6. Ibid, 1:182, 387.
7. Ibid., 2:1361, 225.
8. Harry S. Truman, *Memoirs,* Vol. 1, *Year of Decisions,* (Garden City, N.Y.: Doubleday, 1955), pp. 87, 421, 425.
9. Richard M. Nixon, *The Real War* (New York: Warner Books, 1980), p. 12.

10. Robert F. Kennedy, *Thirteen Days: A Memoir of the Cuban Missile Crisis* (New York: W. W. Norton & Company, 1969), pp. 173, 80.

11. Ibid., pp. 199–200.

12. McGeorge Bundy, "October 27, 1962: Transcripts of the Meeting of the ExComm," *International Security* 12, no. 3 (Winter 1987–88): 30–92.

13. Kennedy, *Thirteen Days*, p. 94.

14. Ibid, p. 109, 106.

15. Robert S. McNamara, "The Lessons of October," *Newsweek*, February 13, 1989, p. 47.

16. Graham Allison, *Essence of Decision* (Boston: Little, Brown & Co., 1979), p. 39; Noam Chomsky, "Strategic Arms, the Cold War & the Third World," in *Exterminism and the Cold War*, ed. *New Left Review* (London: Thetford Press, Ltd., 1983), p. 223.

17. Thomas Powers, "Choosing a Strategy for World War III," *Atlantic Monthly*, November 1982, p. 99.

18. Karl von Clausewitz, *War, Politics, and Powers: Selections from "On War" and "I Believe and Profess,"* trans. and ed. Edward M. Collins (Chicago: Henry Regnery Company, 1962), p. 65.

19. Jonathan Schell, *The Fate of the Earth* (New York: Alfred A. Knopf, 1982), p. 198.

20. Robert Jastrow, *How to Make Nuclear Weapons Obsolete* (Boston: Little, Brown & Co., 1983), p.13.

21. Reported by the Associated Press, April 22, 1990.

22. *Time Magazine*, April 28, 1986, pp. 16–27.

23. "Syria and Terrorism: The Evidence Mounts," *U.S. News and World Report*, May 19, 1986, p. 34.

24. Matt. 7:12; Luke 6:31.

25. A. Russell Buchanan, *The United States and World War II* (New York: Harper and Row, 1964), p. 191.

26. Ronald Reagan, "Peace and National Security," in *Weapons In Space*, ed. Franklin A. Long, et al. (New York: W.W. Norton & Company, 1986), p. 352.

27. Ibid.

28. Mikhail S. Gorbachev, *Toward a Better World* (New York: Richardson & Steirman, 1987), p. 55.

29. Carl Sagan, et al., "Global Atmospheric Consequences of Nuclear War," *Parade Magazine*, October 30, 1983, pp. 4–7.

30. Agreement reached May 18, 1990, reported by Susan Bennett and Fen Montaigne, "Arms Limits Solved," Knight-Ridder Washington Bureau in *Tallahassee Democrat,* May 20, 1990, p. 1A.
31. Mikhail Gorbachev, *Reykjavík: Results & Lessons* (Madison, Conn.: Sphinx Press, Inc.), pp. 16, 21, 47, 22.
32. "Senate Joint Resolution 163: On nuclear weapons freeze and reductions," *Congressional Record,* 97th Cong. 2d sess. (Washington, D.C.: U.S. Government Printing Office), March 10, 1982.
33. Meeting held May 29–June 25, 1988, reported by Kit Pineau and Fergus Watt, *World Federalist News* 8, no. 2, (September 1988).

Part 4: From Enemies to Friends

1. Scott Sullivan, "Big Europe or Little Europe," *Newsweek,* March 12, 1990, p. 38.
2. Clarence K. Streit, *Union Now: A Proposal for a Federal Union of the Democracies of the North Atlantic* (New York: Harper & Brothers Publishers, 1940).
3. David W. Felder, *The Best Investment: Land in a Loving Community* (Tallahassee, Fla.: Wellington Press, 1983).
4. *Tallahassee Democrat,* May 30, 1990.

Part 5: Educating for Peace

1. The Association for Humanistic Psychology, 325 Ninth Street, San Francisco, CA 94103.
2. USSR-USA Friendship Society, 14 Kalinin Avenue, Moscow, 103009, USSR.
3. International Pen Pals, Box 32276, Washington, DC 20007.
4. Esperanto League of North America, P.O. Box 1129, El Cerrito, CA 94530.
5. Grand Admiral von Tirpitz, *My Memoir* (London: Hurst and Blocheth, 1919), pp. 214–42.
6. James McCartney, "Bush Gave Green Light to Saddam," *Tallahassee Democrat,* September 22, 1990, p. 18A; James Baker quoted on NBC's "Meet the Press," September 23, 1990, in an article by Carl P. Leubsdorf, "Statements Invited Saddam

to Make Move on Kuwait," *Tallahassee Democrat,* September 30, 1990, p. 3F.

7. Gordon Feller, et al., eds., *Peace and World Order Studies: A Curriculum Guide* (New York: Transnational Academic Program, Institute for World Order, 1981), p. 79.

8. Daniel C. Thomas, *Guide to Careers and Graduate Education in Peace Studies* (Amherst, Mass.: Hampshire College, The Five-College Program in Peace and World Security Studies, 1987) p. 18.

9. Betty A. Reardon, *Comprehensive Peace Education: Educating for Global Responsibility* (New York: Teachers College Press, 1988), pp. 14, 26.

10. Fran Schmidt and Alice Friedman, *Creative Conflict Solving for Kids;* also books, videos, and posters from The Grace Contrino Abrams Peace Education Foundation, Inc., P.O. Box 191153, Miami Beach, FL 33119, (305)377-8161, ext. 49.

11. International Peace Academy, 777 UN Plaza, New York, NY 10017, (212)949-8480.

12. United States Institute of Peace, 1550 M Street, N.W., Suite 700, Washington, DC 20005-1708, (202)457-1700.

13. Peace Research Institute, 25 Dundana Avenue, Dundas, Ontario, Canada L9H 4E5, (416)628-2356.

14. Consortium on Peace Research, Education, and Development (COPRED), c/o Center for Conflict Resolution, George Mason University, 4400 University Drive, Fairfax, VA 22030, (703)323-2806.

15. For information on mediation games, Wellington Press, Box 13504, Tallahassee, FL 32317.

16. Roger Fisher and William Ury, *Getting to Yes: Negotiating Agreement without Giving In* (New York: Penguin Books, 1983), p. 41.

17. Ibid., p. 87.

18. John von Neumann and Oskar Morgenstern, *Theory of Games and Economic Behavior* (Princeton N.J.: Princeton University Press, 1944).

19. Alan Newcombe, "The Natures of Man and a Pathway to Peace," a paper invited by the International Colloquium on World Peace of the XVII World Congress of Philosophy (Dundas, Ontario, Canada: Peace Research Institute, 1983).

20. Charles Osgood, *An Alternative to War or Surrender* (Urbana: University of Illinois Press, 1962). This particular formulation is found in the preface to the 1970 edition.
21. Amatai Etzioni, "The Kennedy Experiment," *Western Political Quarterly*, 20 (1967): 368–69.
22. Newcombe, *Natures of Man*.

Part 6: Thinking Globally, Acting Locally

1. Common Cause, 2030 M Street, N.W., Washington, DC 20036, (202)833-1200
2. SANE-FREEZE, 711 G Street, S.E., Washington, DC 20009, (202)546-7100
3. Friends Committee on National Legislation (FCNL), 245 Second Street N.E., Washington, DC 20002, (202)547-6000.
4. The conference of thirty-seven experts was organized by the Norwegian branch of the World Association for World Federation which issued a report in July 1989. The recommendation has the endorsement of the Norwegian government and its mission to the United Nations, which is circulating the report to other missions.
5. International Court of Justice (World Court), June 27, 1986, decision by a vote of twelve to three.
6. George Bush, "Transcripts of the Comments by Bush on the Air Strikes against the Iraqis," *New York Times International*, January 17, 1991, p. A14.

Index